Compliments of

B. DALTON, BOOKSELLER
200 KEARNY STREET
SAN FRANCISCO, CALIF.

Grand Opening

Wonders, Warriors, and Beasts Abounding

Dies Solis, detail from *Tapiz de la Creación,* 11th century

WONDERS, WARRIORS, AND BEASTS ABOUNDING

By Beryl Barr

FOREWORD BY THOMAS P. F. HOVING
Director of the Metropolitan Museum of Art

WITH 117 REPRODUCTIONS
31 IN FULL COLOR

Doubleday & Company, Inc., Garden City, New York

To my mother and father

Lines from "New Year Letter" by W. H. Auden (from *Collected Poetry of W. H. Auden*), copyright 1944 by W. H. Auden. Reprinted by permission of Random House, Inc., and Faber and Faber Ltd.

Lines from "Commentary" by W. H. Auden (from *The Collected Poetry of W. H. Auden*), copyright 1945 by W. H. Auden. Reprinted by permission of Random House, Inc., and Faber and Faber Ltd.

Sleeping warrior. Mochican

CONTENTS

ACKNOWLEDGMENTS

I acknowledge with grateful thanks the assistance given to me by various officials of the museums, American and European, represented in this book. In particular I would like to thank Dr. Gordon Ekholm of The American Museum of Natural History, Mr. Wai-kam Ho of the Cleveland Museum of Art, and Mr. Eric Young of the Metropolitan Museum of Art, who each read sections of the text in preparation. For special help I wish to thank Mr. Richard Burton of the Cleveland Museum, Mrs. Dudley Easby, Jr., of the Brooklyn Museum, Miss Louise Houllier of the Pierpont Morgan Library, Miss Elisabeth Little of the Museum of Primitive Art, New York, and Dr. Perry Rathbone, Director of the Museum of Fine Arts, Boston; and in Europe, Mr. Max Antonini of the Schweizerisches Landesmuseum, Zurich, Switzerland; Mr. M. Chatzidakis, Director, and Mrs. Polycharoniadis of the Benaki Museum, Athens, Greece; Mrs. Poly Demoulini of the Agora Museum, American School of Classical Studies, Athens; Mr. George Dontas, Director, Museum of Corfu, Greece; Herr Dr. Hans Fehrlin, Director, Stadtbibliothek (Vadiana), St. Gallen, Switzerland; Herr Dr. Paul Scherrer, Director, Zentralbibliothek, Zurich; and Herr Dr. Wagner of the Berner Kunstmuseum, Berne, Switzerland.

I also wish to acknowledge the assistance in the United States of Miss Virginia Burton and Mrs. Robert Cross of the Metropolitan Museum of Art, Mrs. Wendy Goodell of the Museum of Fine Arts, Boston, Miss Pearl Moeller and Mr. Richard Tooke of the Museum of Modern Art, and Miss Harriet Barr of Los Angeles; and, in Europe, Herr Dr. D. Ahrens of the Staatlichen Antikensammlungen, Munich, Germany; Monsieur Fabré of the Conservation des Musées de Toulouse, France; the Rte. Santos Felipe, Conservador del Tesoro de la Catedral, Gerona, Spain; Mrs. Salvatianon of the National Archaeological Museum, Athens; and Mrs. Renate Winkler of the Graphische Sammlung, Albertina, Vienna, Austria. I also wish to thank Mr. John Levee of Paris for the use of his Jaina Mayan figure, and Mme. Françoise de Staël of Paris for the use of *Moon* by the late Nicolas de Staël.

It would not have occurred to me to write a book for young readers without the suggestion of Mrs. John W. Greenman, and I wish to acknowledge here with warm thanks her invaluable assistance. My thanks go also to Miss Patricia Scigulinsky and Miss Jedy Savage for their efficient secretarial help. To my husband, Roger Barr, I owe special thanks for photographing the *Tapiz de la Creación* in Gerona, the Jaina Mayan figure, and the gargoyle, sarcophagus, and *cul de lampe* from the Musée des Augustins in Toulouse. This special thanks is added to my grateful acknowledgment of his kind and helpful encouragement in this project as in everything I do.

Beryl Barr

FOREWORD

A few familiar and fundamental elements of life as we know it have long served artists as sources of inspiration. Such constants as the sky and its stars above us, the myriad kinds of animals around us, and various images of heroic man lead to our experiencing feelings of joy, fear, wonder, or the like. Impressions of these constants are recorded in the symbols and patterns of myths, legends, religions, private dreams, and works of art. With our remembered experiences and our imaginations we can appreciate art that is separated from us by great geographical distance, thousands of years, baffling language, or exotic custom. No matter how far our scientific knowledge advances, our emotional relationship to the universe remains intensely personal. It is interpreted for us over and over again in art, according to the time and culture in which the art is produced.

In earlier cultures the identity of the artist was rarely essential, since his personal vision was dominated by the conventions of his day. The stylized work of the Egyptians or the Aztecs was prepared in accordance with inflexible traditions, and even today the dying art of icon painting follows a rigid procedure. In societies perhaps more advanced than those I have mentioned, the artist's own feeling and imagination

7

are revealed more freely, yet we can nearly always note influences of the artist's time and place in his creations.

Regardless of their degree of greatness, artists have always played an important role in the lives of men. Some of their products are collected and treasured in museums. Others are perhaps soon forgotten. But even the artist-craftsman, decorating objects of daily need, has continually used themes that concern the society of which he is a member. Designs on plates and patterns in fabric, to mention common examples only, derive from artists' visions, just as other visions lead to the making of great paintings or sculpture. In certain societies an artist's creation will entice or dispel evil spirits—or so it is believed. In others a comparable creation may become a venerated idol. Every age bristles with particular signs and symbols. They bombard our senses, demanding understanding and response.

Works of art are proof of man's ability to react objectively to the world and his place in it. Few of us pursue knowledge of nature with greater fervor or sensitivity than the artist. His special gift is his power to externalize his excitement and insight in an *object,* a work of art, composed from his own repertory of symbols. What he produces is the result of his struggle to deal in some way with the big question: What is the meaning of the universe? This result may be playful, even trivial, or it may be ambitious, wondrous. Whatever the case, some kind of a work of art has come into being. If we ignore it we close our eyes to a measure of human greatness.

THOMAS P. F. HOVING
Director, Metropolitan Museum of Art

8

Tarot card, Italian, 18th century

THE SUN

That sun that warms you here
shall shine on me.

SHAKESPEARE, *Richard II*

What do we see when we look at something as familiar as the sun?
What do we see when we close our eyes to imagine it, or when we
dream? How can we portray it when we wish to share our experience of it with others?

The sun has many faces. Usually, to our eyes, the sun is a luminous circle, high in the sky, hanging like a brilliant lamp. At dawn
or sunset the sun is often a glowing ball of fire; at other times it
is too intensely bright to look at, but it radiates its energy to light
the landscape all around us.

From where we watch it, the sun seems to move across the stage
of the sky from dawn to sunset. We know more than our eyes tell
us, however. We know, through science, that it is the earth which
moves around the sun, and as we move with it our view of the
sun changes. We often feel that the sun is near us. It is actually
very far away, even in summer when it is most brilliant and warm.

What we see and feel about the sun—the perception and experience of it through our senses—differs from our scientific knowledge
of it.

9

Drawing by Anthony de la Cerda, at age 5, Los Angeles, California

Science tells us that the sun is approximately 330,000 times greater in mass than the earth, that the light and heat rays produced by its burning gases travel ninety-three million miles to reach us, that the sun is the source of all energy on earth, and so on. This "true" nature of the sun cannot be demonstrated in a picture of the sun—even a picture by the greatest artist. But the experience of the sun, as well as man's ideas and emotions about it, *can* be expressed.

Most people, when asked to make a picture of the sun, draw a circle or disk with rays indicating heat and light. If they color their picture, they use yellow, orange, or red rather than green or blue. Sunlight at high noon seems to be yellow, and at dawn and sunset it is often red or orange. Yellow, orange, and red are the colors we see most prominently in the flames of a fire. We associate them with heat, and perhaps this is one reason we feel warmer when we look at one of these colors than when we look at green or blue, the colors of cool grass and calm seas.

The child who painted this sun chose yellow, then graced his sun with spectacles, perhaps because of his own response to gazing into the blinding light of a California sun.

The "seven colored sun," a symbol from an alchemical manuscript, *ca.* 1530.

When we make a picture of the sun, we are making both an *image* and a *symbol* of it. An image is a visual likeness, or imitation, of a person or object. An image is also something that is pictured in the mind, or dreamed. A symbol is something that stands for or represents something else and makes visible that which otherwise might not be clearly understood.

Although man's portrayals of the sun have in common the human

11

experience of the same sun, various images differ. They differ according to the time, the culture, and the geographical location in which the artist lives. They also differ according to the ability of the individual artist to transform what his senses and intellect tell him, into a picture which will express something to other men.

If the artist gives his disk-and-rays symbol of the sun a human face, he may express how he feels about the sun, or how he wishes us to feel, or both. Most people seem to think the sun "smiles," and so they give it a happy face. The idea of a "laughing" sun, like the disk-and-rays, is a conventional symbol—a symbol used so often that it is understood by almost everyone.

The sun is not always friendly, however. It has great powers of destruction. It can cause drought and desert, and in tropical climates its intense heat contributes to certain diseases. This dual role of the sun—its magnificent life-giving nature and its power to destroy—inspired primitive man with both reverence and fear.

Since the beginning of recorded history, the sun has been a source of awe for all men. It has inspired poetry and art, and for centuries it was one of the most widely worshiped gods in mythology and religion.

The sun is still considered a god in certain primitive societies in New Zealand and Africa, where the bushmen in the deserts of the south pray to it. In towns in remote parts of Europe, men raise their hats in greeting and homage to the rising sun, following a custom centuries old. An old German custom forbids pointing at the sun because it was once considered harmful to point at something or someone. Certainly no one wished to threaten the sun.

In Japan people continue a custom of welcoming the sun in

Wood engraved vignette, 17th century

12

the morning by clapping hands. In parts of Russia the peasants call upon the sun to avenge a wrong. "May the sun make you perish," they say to someone to whom they wish ill. And in parts of Europe hunters practice the old custom of shooting at the rising sun for good luck in the hunt. The sun is believed to have magic properties, which indeed it has.

Thousands of years ago in ancient Egypt a falcon was the symbol of the sky. Those who took the symbol literally believed that the sun was the right eye of the sky-falcon, and the moon was his left eye. The falcon opened only one eye at a time, thus creating day and night at different times, according to this theory.

The ancient Egyptians believed the sun they saw above them ruled the earth. As a powerful god, he was worshiped under several different names, according to his position in the sky and his particular role at the time of worship. When the sun was high in the sky he was called the god Ra. He was Khepera when he rose in the east, and Atum when he set. He was also called Ra Harakhti and sometimes Horus. Finally, for a brief period under the reign of the King Akhenaton, about 1300 B.C., the names and legends merged into one, and the sun god became known as the Aten. During the short duration of the cult of the Aten, Akhenaton built a new capital city to the glory of the solar disk. In the solar temple, ceremonies were held glorifying the sun as the creator of mankind.

Although the Egyptians had some knowledge of the stars and assigned astronomers to their temples, myths explaining the movements of the sun they observed remained primitive. The Egyptians believed that the sun traveled from east to west through the sky in a barque or boat which resembled their own Nile riverboats. Since the Egyptians lived in the valley of the Nile, the boat seemed to them a natural and convenient means of transportation. When the sun disappeared every evening after the hours of light, it became a passenger in a special "night" barque for the journey through the waters of the dark underworld. The sun faced great dangers during his passage through the underworld. But with the help of the sun god Ra who accompanied him, all dangers were overcome and at last the sun greeted the inhabitants of the underworld who had waited impatiently for the light he bore them.

The sun reappeared every morning and made his journey across the sky. The only threat to his safety during the day was that of being swallowed, partially or whole, by his perpetual enemy, the great river serpent Apophis. Apophis rarely managed to swallow

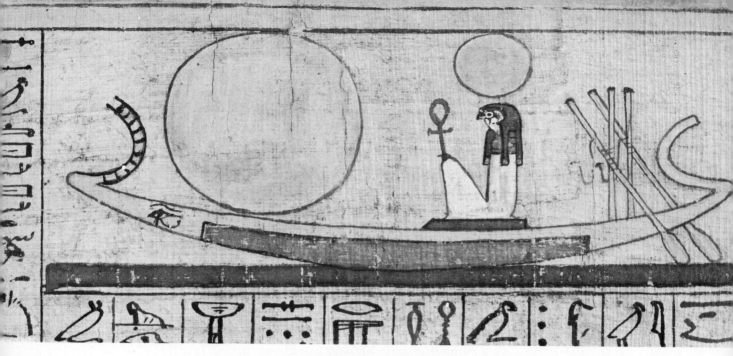

Ra, the Egyptian sun god

the sun, as Ra went to great trouble to help the sun avoid the monster. But when it did happen—thereby causing an eclipse of the sun—the divine barque always managed to escape.

This drawing on papyrus (paper made from the papyrus reeds which grow in the Nile River) shows the god Ra with the sun as his precious charge in the special barque. It was drawn more than three thousand years ago. The sun is shown as a simple disk. Another disk forms the headdress of the falcon-headed god of the sun himself. Ra sits very solemnly, holding on his knees the Egyptian symbol of life. It indicates that, as a god, he is not subject to the death of ordinary mortals. Thousands of years later, the Incas of ancient Peru (which included more of the South American continent than does modern Peru today) worshiped the sun and named it Inti. They represented the face of the sun with a disk of gold surrounded by rays.

The Incas thought that Inti plunged into the sea at evening and swam under the earth all night long. He returned the next morning, refreshed by his bath, ready for the day's journey across the sky.

The Aztecs of ancient Mexico, too, considered the sun a powerful god. They thought the sun demanded sacrificial blood, perhaps because it appeared and disappeared every day in a flush of red dawn and sunset, and they sacrificed countless victims to it. Otherwise, the Aztecs believed, the sun might not return to them every morning, or it would return in anger, bringing great heat and harmful drought.

On the next page is the Aztec sun god Tonatiuh. He wears a sun disk. The Aztecs greatly feared their sun god and therefore presented him in terrifying guise. Like Ra, the Aztec sun god had different names to indicate his many aspects. One of the names was Tezcatlipoca, which means "smoking mirror." Tezcatlipoca was the summer sun which parched and burned the land. He sometimes appeared to men in the form of a flying shadow, or a monster, but his symbol was a mirror with flames coming from it.

Priests and artists of both the ancient Egyptian and the Aztec civilizations had established official images of the sun and the sun god long before these two pictures were made. In both cases, the picture of the sun god reflects a whole civilization's beliefs about the sun. The artist of the Egyptian papyrus drawing followed rules which told him how Ra should be depicted in order to be recognized by everyone in his culture. These rules were developed and sometimes modified over the more than three thousand years of the Egyptian civilization. The Egyptian artist was not expressing his own personal experience of the sun; he was portraying the religious belief of an entire culture.

Similarly, it was important for the Aztec artist to present the god exactly as the people believed he looked, and to represent correctly the ceremonial aspects of Tonatiuh's power. That is why various symbols of ceremonies in which the god was assumed to take part are included on his garments and around his picture.

In both the Egyptian and Aztec cultures, the sun and the sun gods (who were distinct beings from the sun itself) were personified, or given human characteristics. This was true in many other civilizations in which the need and imagination of the people helped them create a special god whose function was to safeguard the sun.

Shamash, the sun god of Assyro-Babylonian mythology, was believed to have the form of a man with luminous rays streaming off his shoulders like wings. As the "Judge of the Heavens and the Earth" who triumphed over darkness, he was considered both courageous and just. Portrayed in his role of judge, Shamash is seen sitting on a throne with a scepter and ring in his right hand.

The Greeks, too, personified the sun and named it Helios. Helios arose every morning in the east at the sound of the cock's crow, and in a golden chariot drawn by dazzling white horses, he sped across the sky to light the world. The horses were winged and breathed fire through their nostrils.

When the day was over Helios seemed to plunge into the

15

Tonatiuh, the Aztec sun god

wears a sun disk

Helios Rising, Greek plate

sea, but every Greek knew that he was really met by a golden ferry boat in which his mother, wife, and children waited for him. With them he traveled all night to arrive at the point of his departure for the new day's journey through the sky. His chariot and horses traveled with him on the ferry.

Helios saw and knew everything because he shed light on men and gods alike. Nothing could be hidden from him. He discovered and revealed many of the tricks that the Greek gods were fond of playing on one another, and according to Greek mythology, he apparently caused as much trouble telling on the misdoers as would have resulted had he remained silent.

But although Helios was a tattletale, he was very courteous. When Herakles was working to fulfill one of the twelve labors which had been imposed upon him that he might find immortality with the gods, Helios the sun was burning so brightly and hotly in the sky that Herakles found it impossible to work. In a fit of temper he shot an arrow at the sun. Helios cried out in anger, and Herakles apologized. Helios accepted his apology, and to show his forgiveness he lent Herakles his golden goblet, shaped like a water lily.

17

In it, Herakles sailed off on the ocean to the island of Erytheia where his tenth labor was to fetch the beautiful red cattle of Geryon, a monster with three heads, six hands, and three bodies joined at the waist.

Helios had many sons, some of whom became astronomers, which was not surprising considering their father's occupation. However, one of the sons, named Phaethon, did not have a distinguished career. After much persuasion, Phaethon obtained his father's promise to allow him to drive the chariot of the sun for a day. But he was not strong enough to check the powerful white horses and they first went so high in the sky that everyone on earth shivered, then so close to the earth that the fields scorched and burned as the chariot passed. In order to save the world from going up in flames, Zeus, the king of the gods, flung a thunderbolt at the unruly Phaethon and he fell from the chariot into the River Po.

The image of a sun god with a chariot has long been a popular symbol for the sun. Even before Helios, the fiery-winged Assyro-Babylonian god Shamash emerged every morning from the tallest of the mountains of the east and, climbing up to the very top, met his coachman busy harnessing the great chariot of the sun. In a dazzle of early morning light, Shamash slowly drove his chariot up into the sky and then across it to banish the darkness and bring men day. At evening Shamash guided his chariot toward the highest mountain in the west and disappeared behind it. All night he traveled underground to reach the east again.

In Polish folktales still told today the sun rides in a diamond chariot pulled by twelve golden-maned horses. In other old European legends, the sun has three horses: one silver, one diamond, and one gold. In these legends the sun lives in a glorious palace in the east from which his chariot rises with each new dawn.

A sun god is represented in a tapestry on the frontispiece of this book. A tapestry is a cloth woven on warps, or threads stretched on a loom, by a craftsman who passes many colored threads, or wefts, over and under the warps to form a pattern. This tapestry was made in Spain in the eleventh century, and tells a story from the Bible, the story of creation. *Dies Solis* means "day of the sun." The Spanish artist or artisan who designed the tapestry borrowed the idea of a sun god from pagan religions and placed it in a Christian context. As a personified image, it represents the sun which God created on the third day:

18

> And God made two great lights;
> the greater light to rule the day,
> and the lesser light to rule the night:
> he made the stars also.

GENESIS 1:16

The sun god sits in his chariot, holding in his lap the globe of the sun, a symbol of his function. Around his head he wears the rays of the sun. The tiny horses pulling his chariot run up the side of the circle that encloses them as if to indicate their encircling trip around the earth.

The *Dies Solis* is one fragment, or detail, of the whole tapestry, just as the creation of the sun is only one part of the story of creation as it is told in the Book of Genesis.

In almost every known mythology and religion the sun plays a very important role. From the worship of the sun and its light, a great variety of interesting gods have emerged. In the mythology of the early Germanic peoples, one of the most important gods was Heimdall, the god of light. One of his duties was to guard the rainbow, the bridge which led from the world of men to that of the gods, and he was usually found near a rainbow. He slept very little and could see at night as easily as during the day. He had teeth of pure gold.

The Greek god of light was Apollo. He was a kind of sun god without being, like Helios, the personification of the sun itself. Apollo had a great many duties. He protected crops, banished illness, and was the god of music and prophecy. He was called the "bright one" and is depicted in Greek art as a beautiful young man.

The Indian sun god Surya was so dazzling that his wife Sanjna was forced to leave him until his father-in-law reduced his brilliance by one-eighth and Sanjna could bear to look at him again. The Indian manuscript on the next page shows Surya in his chariot with the brilliant nimbus, or halo of his power.

The shrine of the Japanese sun goddess Amaterasu contains a sacred mirror. It is said to be the mirror which lured her out of the cave in which she had once hidden her radiance. When Amaterasu is worshiped at the shrine, her spirit is assumed to enter the mirror.

The Slavic god Dazhbog was both the god of the sun and the god of happiness.

We can see how symbols of the sun become part of the personalities of the sun gods. The various gods are associated with the

Surya, the Indian sun god

rainbow, dazzling light, the mirror—which reflects light—and happiness, which the sun is thought to give us.

It is the experience of sunlight, its brilliance and its warmth,
which man senses and symbolizes in a creative way, whether in his
religion, his dreams, or his art. The true nature of the sun cannot

be shown in painting, or sculpture, or tapestry. How could the artist attempt to truly depict the sun after the Greek philosopher Anaxagoras insisted it was really a mass of burning metal larger than the southern half of Greece? As modern science grew, so did man's knowledge of the sun. But the ancient and profound emotional relationship of man to the sun has continued, and new expressions of it continue to appear.

> I have been satisfied with my work since the day
> I realized that the sun cannot be portrayed, but
> must be represented by another medium, by color.
> PAUL CÉZANNE

Paul Cézanne was a contemporary of the group of nineteenth-century French painters who were called the Impressionists. Influenced to some extent by their ideas about color, though not a member of the group, Cézanne, as quoted above, could have been speaking for them. The Impressionists were especially concerned with the presentation of sunlight in painting by the use of pure, clear color.

The Impressionists painted scenes of daily life, mostly out-of-doors, and scenes of nature. They studied the tricks that sunlight plays on the foliage of trees and rippling waves of water. They painted with the excitement of direct, personal observation, flooding their paintings with brilliant sunlight and putting color everywhere.

The painting on the next page, *Poplars on the Bank of the Epte River,* is by one of the most important members of the group, Claude Monet. It was painted when Monet had developed Impressionism to its maturity. Sunlight is represented by patches of pure color which shimmer and vibrate over the entire surface of the canvas. Light comes through the trees, intensifying their colors and casting vivid reflections onto the vibrating surface of the river below.

For Vincent Van Gogh, a Dutch artist who also lived during the nineteenth century, the sun had a deeply personal, almost religious significance. When Van Gogh was in the sunny climate of the south of France, he painted many of his finest pictures. He considered the sun a major source of his inspiration.

> I have a terrible lucidity at moments, when nature
> is so glorious in those days I am hardly conscious
> of myself and the picture comes to me like in a
> dream. . . . Oh! Those who don't believe in this
> sun here are real infidels.
> THE LETTERS OF VINCENT VAN GOGH

22

Claude Monet (1840–1926). *Poplars on the Bank of the Epte River*, 1891

burning sun *yellow*

Vincent Van Gogh (1853–1890). *Wheatfield with Reaper*

Many of Van Gogh's paintings are vibrant with a glowing yellow. He painted yellow skies, golden sunflowers, and yellow cornfields under the burning sun. For Van Gogh, nature was not the civilized, domesticated part of daily life that it was for the Impressionists. The sun was a powerful force in the turbulent nature he saw, felt, and painted. This painting, *Wheatfield with Reaper*, shows the sun as a yellow disk in the sky. The painting is filled with shimmering lines of color like rays of energy in flux and flow.

Even when he was not using color, Van Gogh nevertheless managed to impart a sense of the shimmering, vibrating quality of light. The undulating lines of his drawings pulse with energy, indicating with every stroke of the pen the constant movement of

23

NO COLOR
sense of the shimmering
(vibrating) light

Vincent Van Gogh (1853–1890). *View from the Hospital*

undulating line
pulsive energy

nature as the artist saw and felt it. Above, the sun radiates energy, dominating the entire drawing with its power to give things life.

The beloved radiance of the sun has been suggested by means of line in a sculpture of fine gold wire by a contemporary American artist, Richard Lippold. The photograph of the sculpture resembles a mirror image, but Lippold's sun is not just a reflection.

This sculpture is made out of thousands of gold wires. The wires seem to form a central core of heat and light streaming from the sun, giving us a striking sense of its glow and brilliance. The warmth of the sun is suggested, when we actually see the sculpture,

24

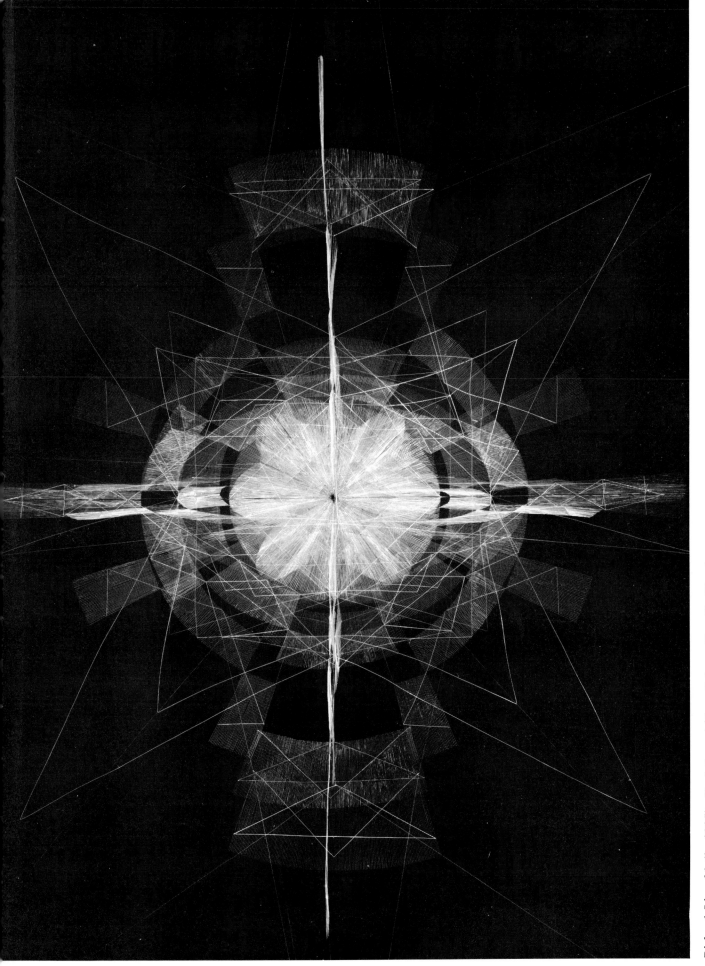

Richard Lippold (b. 1915). *Variation within a Sphere, No. 10: The Sun*

by the yellow-gold color of the wires. Lippold also made a sculpture of the moon. It is made of silver because the light of the moon is reflected light and does not give us heat.

A French artist named Robert Delaunay was interested in the pure colors of sunlight. Rather than depict the experience of the sun in terms of the colors it gave the landscape around him, as the Impressionists had done, Delaunay chose to work with sunlight's pure colors in an *abstract* form.

When an artist abstracts an object, he takes from the object that part or shape or color of it which is of particular interest to him, and transforms it while he is painting. He transforms it into something which may suggest the original object, but which has a special new life and meaning of its own.

Delaunay took the circle or disk, which as we have seen is the simplest and most widely understood symbol for the sun, together with the pure colors of sunlight, to make an abstraction. If he had an interest in the magic and energy of the sun, his was not an emotional response like Van Gogh's, but an intellectual one. Delaunay was more interested in the rhythm and expressive power of colors as they acted one against the other than he was in expressing his own personal experience of the sun, or sunlight.

This painting by Delaunay is entitled *Solar Discs*. It is obvious that here the artist is not representing what he sees when he looks at the sun, but is, instead, expressing an idea about color and round shapes which by their nature relate to the sun.

All artists who use color are interested in the way colors work together and in their expressive power. The expressive power of a color is how it makes us *feel* when we see it. We have referred to "warm" and "cool" colors. "Warm" colors are considered more emotionally exciting than "cool" colors. Just as a warm and friendly person comes toward us to make us feel at ease, so "warm" colors seem to come forward from the flat surface of a picture. Similarly, "cool" colors, like blue and blue-green, seem to recede or withdraw like a distant sky.

The power of colors to move back and forth in space is part of their interaction. How colors look beside each other is another concern of painters. Formal arrangements of colors sometimes depend upon such visual judgments as whether to have colors "clash" in an exciting way or balance in more quiet harmony. There are no rules about using color, but most artists try to find a kind of color *relatedness,* or unity, in their painting.

not representing what he sees

Robert Delaunay (1885–1941). *Solar Discs*

27

Imaji Takeshi (b. 1913). *Sun*

This abstraction, drawn in line alone, is based on the Chinese
sign or "character" for the sun. Chinese writing expresses ideas
through abstract pictures rather than words formed by letters. For
"sun," the ancient Chinese drew a circle with a dot in it. Later this
was modified into a character resembling a ladder. This screen,
with the characters for "sun" drawn in a free and personal way,
becomes significant as a decorative and symbolically meaningful
work of art.

Ancient Japanese crests

In contrast to the free and fluid line of the Chinese characters, the shapes of these Japanese sun designs used for family crests seem as rigidly and mathemetically formed as shapes punched out by a machine. Nevertheless, there is an elegance to the artful arrangements of their simplified forms.

Astrology is the study of stars and planets on given days in the belief that their relative positions and movements affect events on earth.

On the next page an Indian goddess symbolically carries the sun on its journey through that period of the year governed, in astrology, by Leo the lion: July 21–August 22. The lion's body is made up of

29

Indian manuscript leaf, 17th–18th centuries

animals and figures. Compare this painting to the Indian miniature of Surya on page 20.

For Joan Miro, a contemporary Spanish artist, the sun has meaning here as a symbol placed in an unexpected context. The title of this picture tells us that the figure has gobbled up the sun.

Amusing absurd relocation, out of usual context

relationship to sun intensely personal

direct quality

bold vigorous figure playful

another world fantasy shared

sun

stomach

colors (pure) colorful decorative black pattern flat

inspired by wild freeness expressed around him

Joan Miro (b. 1893). *Sun-Eater*

expresses our poetry in dreams myths

sun — symbol placed in unexpected context figure has gobbled up the sun

31

We can see the sun—the familiar red disk symbol—very clearly in the figure's stomach. Miro has brought the sun down out of its place of glory in the sky and placed it in an amusing and absurd situation. It glows with a brilliant red warmth.

The colors of this painting are arranged in a decorative pattern on the surface. Miro's colors are the same pure colors (plus black) which interested Delaunay, but here they are used flat, and in brilliant hues. We see at once that Miro painted on a flat, even surface, giving the painting a direct quality. The figure, a playful image, presents itself to us boldly and vigorously. The painting seems to suggest another world, a world of the artist's fantasy which he allows us to share through the humor and good nature of his vision.

Miro's world, into which we enter each time we look at a Miro painting, is a world of the artist's imagination. Though inspired by what he experiences around him, Miro expresses his own particular poetry in a language which deals in dreams and myths.

Modern artists' depictions of the sun, such as Miro's humorous and poetic one or Van Gogh's intensely felt responses, are as interpretive and magical as the mythological symbols of a far more primitive people. Miro, Van Gogh, and other artists show us that no matter how much scientists probe and analyze the sun to increase our knowledge, our relationship to the sun can always remain, on some level, intensely personal.

Flemish manuscript, 13th century

A
BESTIARY

The animal kingdom, sharing the earth with man, is more easily observed than the remote and mysterious sun.

Animals in art are as old as art itself. Prehistoric man scratched or painted likenesses of the animals he needed for food on the walls of his cave, hoping that the "magic" quality of the images would help his hunt. Together with primitive symbols for the sun, these are the oldest examples of art that are preserved for us.

Animals are the first subject matter of representational or realistic art: that art which attempts a more truly descriptive portrayal than is possible of the sun. Animal shapes and forms have been popular with artists and craftsmen of all cultures. They are often used to decorate objects, such as pottery and fabrics.

Men have observed animals carefully, portraying them in sculpture, line, and color, and describing them in words. There are many stories and fables about animals, and animal parables in the Bible are considered positive examples of how man himself should live. "Go to the ant, thou sluggard;" one parable advises, "consider her ways and be wise."

Many artists have illustrated stories from the Bible. The illustration on page 35, from a tenth-century manuscript, is an artist's

33

idea of the second dream of Nebuchadnezzar, king of Babylon in the sixth century B.C., as it is related in the Old Testament. Nebuchadnezzar dreamed that there was a large tree that sheltered all the birds and beasts of the world.

> The leaves thereof were fair,
> and the fruit thereof much,
> and in it was meat for all:
> the beasts of the field had shadow under it,
> and the fowls of the heaven dwelt in the boughs thereof,
> and all flesh was fed of it.
> DANIEL 4:12

The tree in the painting is full of birds. The "beasts" are represented by an ox. At the right is Nebuchadnezzar himself, sheltered by the tree, munching on leaves. For it was Nebuchadnezzar's fate, predicted in the same dream and interpreted by Daniel, to be driven for a time from men "to eat grass as oxen . . . his heart changed from man's and . . . a beast's heart . . . given unto him" until he extolled and honored the "King of Heaven."

Most often man has chosen to portray ordinary animals, but his ability to imagine combinations of the animals he knows has resulted in some bizarre and fabulous creatures.

The ancient Greeks depicted their heroes in battle with monsters like the chimera, who was part lion, part goat, and part serpent. Other fantastic creatures in Greek mythology are the satyr, who was half goat and half man, Pegasus, the winged horse, and the centaur, who had a horse's body and the torso and head of a man.

The sphinx of the Egyptians, with the body of a lion and a Pharaoh's head, was transformed by the Greeks into a winged lion with the head and breasts of a woman. Sculptures were made of the Greek sphinx, and she was often portrayed on pottery.

Harpies were monsters with the face of an old hag, the ears of a bear, the body of a bird, and long, hooked claws. At first, sirens were also represented in Greek art as creatures with a woman's head and the body of a bird. Later they were depicted as mermaids, their bodies ending in fish tails.

The Assyrians carved winged bulls into their palace gates to guard against evil spirits. They also believed that sculpted genies with human bodies and the heads of lions would drive away the demons of disease. The ancient Persians designed winged lions and griffins—creatures with an eagle's head and wings and the sleek body of a lion—in the colorful tiles of their palace walls.

34

Spanish manuscript, 10th century

The variety of animals is enormous, and many animals are quite unlike any other. In a sense, the nature of every animal has special meaning in the scheme of the natural world. The earliest gods of the Egyptians were represented as animals and birds. The animal with which each god was associated endowed that god with its own particular nature. Later the gods were represented as at least partly human—with human bodies and animal or bird heads. We have already encountered Ra, the falcon-headed god of the sun.

35

The falcon was probably related to the sky because of its sweeping flight.

Sekhmet, the Egyptian goddess of war and battle, had the head of a lioness. There was also a bull god, whose birthday was celebrated, a ram god, and even a crocodile god. The crocodile god lived in his own sanctuary in a lake at Crocodilopolis. He was very old and wore golden rings in his ears.

Even today the people who live on the south shore of Lake Victoria Nyanza in Africa keep a crocodile named Lutembi as a sort of deity. Every morning and evening Lutembi comes to the shore for the fish brought by the fishermen in offering.

In West Africa certain tribes take part in a cult of the leopard. In one tribe, anyone who accidentally kills a leopard risks being put to death; in another, a crown of royalty is placed upon the head of a dead leopard and dances are held in its honor.

Creatures as unlikely as objects of worship as the praying mantis and the caterpillar are honored in Africa. The bushmen consider these animals incarnations of one of their gods.

In several mythologies gods were able to assume animal form at will. Zeus, supreme god of the Greek divinities, changed himself at various times into a bull, a swan, a cuckoo bird, and an eagle. Occasionally, too, he became an inanimate object such as a flame or a shower of gold coins.

In early Germanic mythology, a god named Woden-Odin enjoyed the privilege of becoming a bird, a bull, or a snake. He surrounded himself with animals. Two wolves were his pets, and he rode on the swiftest of all stallions.

These animals were portrayed in 1486, six years before Columbus discovered America, by an artist who, together with a German writer named Breydenbach, produced one of the earliest travel books known. The travelers journeyed to Palestine and these are the animals they said they saw there. The drawing was carved into a wood block and then printed. The inscription reads: "These animals are truly depicted as actually seen by us in the Holy Land." The animals are a giraffe, a dromedary camel, a crocodile, an Indian goat, a salamander, an ape whose name the author says he does not know, and a unicorn!

The unicorn lives only in mythology and the legendary romances of the Middle Ages, so the travelers could not really have seen one. But because they considered the unicorn an exotic animal, and

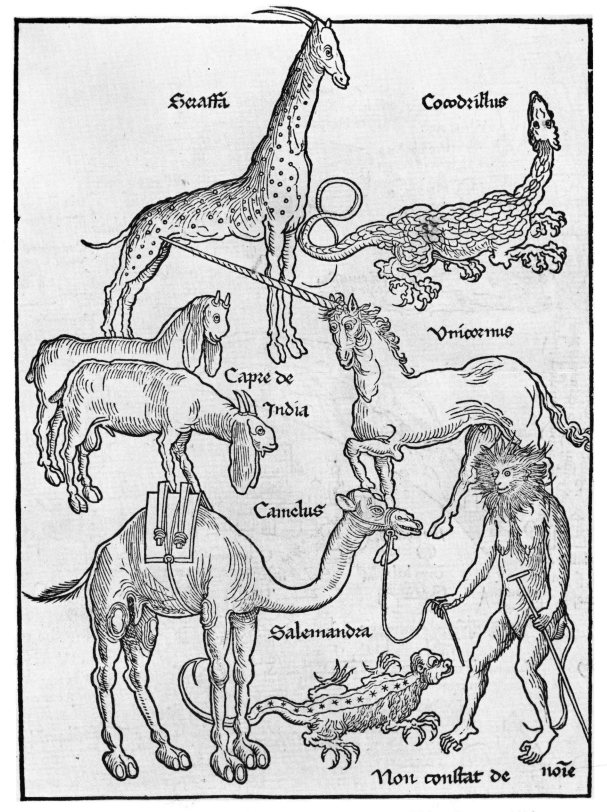

Page from Breydenbach's *Peregrinations in Terram Sanctum.* Mainz, Germany, 1486

Palestine an exotic place, they probably reasoned that if the unicorn existed at all, surely he existed in Palestine. They could therefore include him in their picture, along with the other animals, without the risk of having their faculties of observation challenged!

37

Peruvian tapestry. Nazca-style, *ca.* 300–500

The characteristics which we believe certain animals have are symbols of corresponding qualities in man. Belief in these basic characteristics seems to be almost universal. They appear in fables, mythology, and in various parables in Christian Scripture. The cat is considered cunning and intelligent, the serpent devious, the donkey stupid, the cock vain, the dove harmless, the sheep vulnerable, the owl wise, the deer shy, the fox sly, and the frog—like many birds— talkative and often a little silly.

Perhaps, then, it is not surprising if the busy activity of the birds portrayed here suggests to us a certain amount of noise. This painted cloth was made in Peru more than one thousand years ago. The birds form a decorative, lively pattern.

On the following pages are four birds. Two are from primitive cultures known to us, one is from an unknown culture, and one is

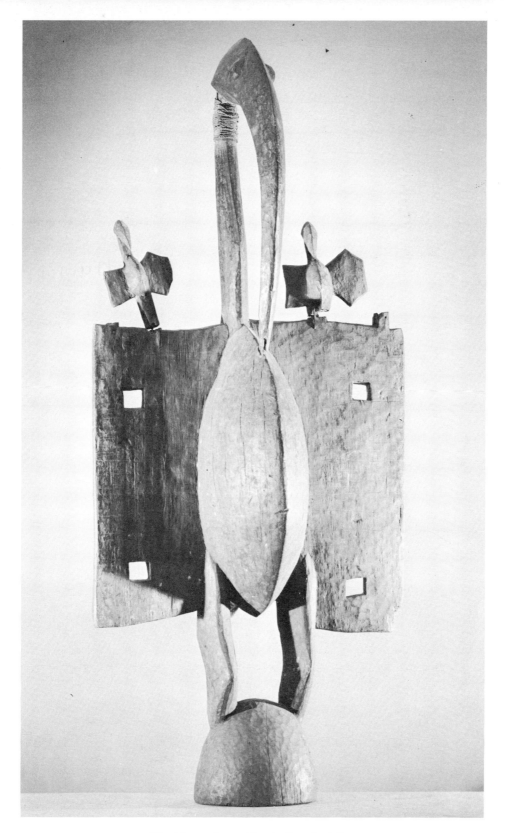

Headdress. Ivory Coast: Senufo tribe

by a modern sculptor. In each case the true *shape* of the bird has been simplified, or abstracted, by using a geometric form.

This African bird has wings in the shape of a rectangle.

40

Bird. N. E. New Guinea

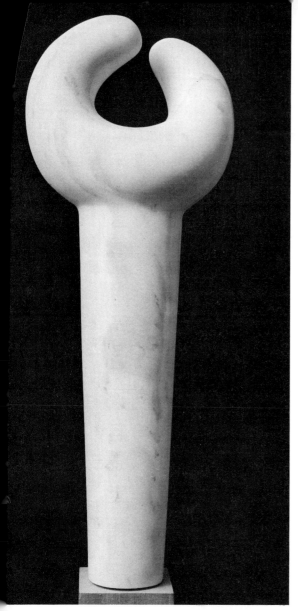

Isamu Noguchi (b. 1904). *Bird C, (Mu)*   Bird (provenance unknown)

The body of the decorated bird from New Guinea is a fat circle.

The modern bird by Isamu Noguchi is a cylinder of marble topped with an open partial circle or crescent, suggesting the opened beak of a bird.

The stone bird looking back toward its tail is perhaps the most realistic or "real" looking of the birds, although it is also simplified. Here, the geometric shape is a triangle. The carved inverted pyramid of the body of the bird (it could be nothing else) shows the slight indication of a wing.

These sculptures are similar in that in each case a bird is depicted. They are all very much like birds, even the abstract marble sculpture by Noguchi, although we might have to be told the title the artist had given his sculpture before seeing *why* it is like a bird.

41

Paul Klee (1879–1940). *Waterbirds*

humor

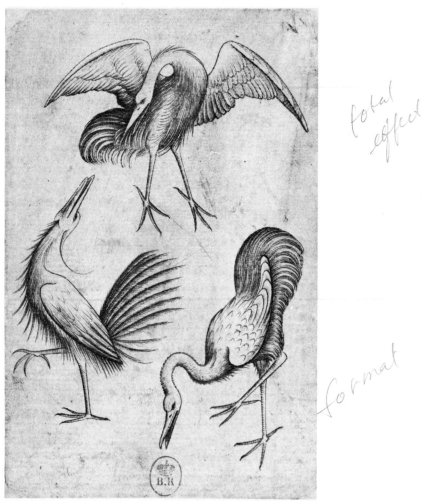

total effect

format

Master of the Playing Cards. Bird Study in ink

Artists through the ages have been concerned with clarity of design. Here we can contrast a twentieth-century artist's drawing of waterbirds with a seventeenth-century drawing. In their flat, abstracted shapes, Paul Klee's birds have the generalized simplicity of

42

Cat. Egyptian

the sculptures on the preceding pages. In the attitude of the birds' heads and the feet on the bird to the right, Klee has suggested humor. The water is just three simple lines on the left and two on the right, as the bird paddling his feet stirs up a wave behind him. What else adds humor to the drawing?

The finely executed drawing by the Master of the Playing Cards, an artist known only by that name, is very formal. We sense the artist's keen powers of observation and his wish to achieve an authenticity to nature. At the same time, the careful positioning of the many studies of the same species of bird indicate that the artist was very aware of the total effect of his design.

Here and on the next two pages are three animals, the cat, the camel, and the cock, all sculpted in different materials at different times in very different cultures. The cat is ancient Egyptian and carved in wood, the camel is baked clay, or terra-cotta, from the Chinese T'ang culture of the seventh and eighth centuries, and the bronze cock is Moslem of the sixteenth century.

How are they similar? First, they are all sculpted in the round, that is, the sculptor has carved or moulded his material to form the back and sides, as well as the front, of the figure. Second, they are each descriptive of the kind of animal they represent; we could not mistake them for different animals. Third, although they are

43

descriptive of the animal they represent, in each case there is a simplification of the animal's shape which makes each sculpture to some extent abstract.

The cat sits up very tall with his forepaws raised on a little platform and his forelegs perfectly straight, forming a rigid line. It is difficult if not impossible to find such a straight line in nature. But it is this, together with the proud attitude of the head and the straight line of the stomach, which give the cat such a great sense of dignity. The Egyptian artist was portraying an animal sacred to his culture. Cats in Egypt were carefully protected and given special burial when they died.

The camel is kneeling (camels often kneel to be loaded and unloaded of their burdens), and in this case it is the exaggerated curve of the neck and back which gives the animal his special character. From his tail to the top of his head the camel's body forms an "S." The smaller curve of the "S" is the lower one, formed by his neck. This curve acts as a kind of spring which might help the camel to his feet if the figure could get up and walk away. It gives

Camel. Chinese, 7th–8th centuries

44

the camel *animation,* or a sense of life. At the same time we realize that because the curve is exaggerated, the figure is to some extent abstract. T'ang sculpture is recognized by this remarkable combination of realistic and abstract qualities which gives the clay figures such a sense of life.

The cock is animated by the thrust of his head. Every line in the sculpture is simplified, and the patterns these lines form have a regularity we would not find in a real cock. His tail feathers are simplified, as is his comb. The wattle under his beak has become a perfect circle. The cock has a quality which we call *stylization* because of these repeated, design-like patterns. The cock is cast in bronze, a hard material which allows the detail of design so often found in Moslem art.

In each example—the cat, the camel, and the cock—we sense the artist's awareness of the true or descriptive nature of the animal, and his ability to simplify it. At the same time we can recognize qualities which make the sculpture an unmistakable product of each artist's own time and culture.

Cock. Moslem, 16th century

Coin. Greek, 5th century B.C. (enlarged about 3 times)

David Hare (b. 1917). *Crab*

46

Tapiz de la Creación (detail). 11th century

On the opposite page are two examples of the same animal. The coin was made in Greece during the fifth century B.C. The standing crab was designed by a modern sculptor. They are both made of metal.

The crab on the coin is a *bas-relief*, that is, the image of the animal is raised slightly above the flatter surface of the background. The tall, standing crab is a sculpture in the round. The exaggeration of the length of the legs adds humor to the figure; the placement of the legs suggests movement. This crab has only three claws. How else does he differ from the crab on the Greek coin?

Above is a detail of the Spanish tapestry, *Tapiz de la Creación*, in which the *Dies Solis* appears (frontispiece). This is a fragment of the creation of the birds and fishes. The crustacean is seen from above, just as the crab on the coin. We cannot be sure that the Spanish craftsman intended this to be a crab, but he has shown it in the way it can be most easily identified as a shelled, many-legged sea animal. It could be a crawfish, or even a lobster.

47

Bowl. New Mexican

The nature of fish is to swim, and to glide with currents of water. The shapes of all of these fish suggest movement of some sort. The two checkered fish with bared teeth seem to be swimming the breast stroke, chasing each other around and around the bowl. We know they will never catch each other, but if we look intently at them for a few moments the whole bowl seems to spin. This illusion is helped by the fact that the bowl is round, like a wheel. An illusion is something that *appears* to be true. The roundness of the bowl is repeated by the stripes around the rim. The dark points inside the rim become like waves in the imaginary sea in which these fish play.

The modern marble fish, a sculpture in the round, is boldly simplified. It has no flippers or other apparent means of propelling itself forward, but nevertheless it suggests the possibility of movement. Consider its shape. We can see that the modern artist has suggested a fish—the curve of its back, its nose, and its tail. This is very much like a real fish in that it would seem not to resist the movement of the sea. We can imagine such a shape gliding quietly along in a current of water in a way that we cannot imagine a solid square or a rectangle gliding.

Brancusi's fish is narrow, only a few inches at the widest point. Because it is placed on its base, or pedestal, just at the point of visual balance, the fish seems light even though it is made of heavy material. It seems capable, if it were given the chance in some world where art comes to life, of *acting* like a fish. The grain of the marble forms delicate white lines. They run with the direction of the fish's movement, just as streams of water flow off a real fish's back as it swims.

48

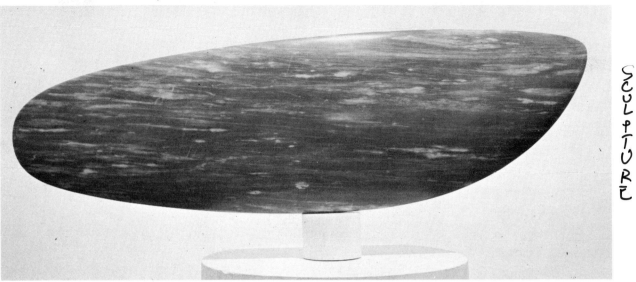

Constantin Brancusi (1876–1957). *Fish*

PURITY – PRECISION

Whale. Vancouver Islands: Kwakiutl Indians

The Northwest Indian whale has powerful-looking flippers and a strong tail. It is not difficult to imagine him flipping his tail and diving through the water. The strength of the tail fin is suggested not only by its size, but by the graceful curve of the back which gives the tail a whiplike quality.

Each of these objects was made for a different reason. The New Mexican Indians designed the bowl for a specific purpose. Brancusi made his fish solely as a piece of sculpture, to be appreciated for its purity and precision as a work of art. The Canadian Indians, perhaps thinking their whale had magic powers, used it as a mask in certain ceremonies. The lower jaw is on a hinge and the whale is painted with vivid patterns.

Yet despite the different functions of these inanimate objects, the artistic use of the fish theme and shape gives to each a sense of potential activity.

49

Alexander Calder (b. 1898). *Whale*

This modern metal whale, like Brancusi's marble fish, is abstract. Its movement is perhaps easier to see and at the same time more difficult to explain in terms of its relationship to organic parts of a real animal. It does not have a whale's shape, though the curves and the black color suggest a whale rather than a fish. To anyone who has seen a porpoise jump, this sculpture is more meaningful.

The picture made from pasted shapes of colored paper is entitled *The Snail*. It is called a *collage* from the French word *coller,* which means to paste, or glue. Here the movement of the almost square shapes defines a circular motion. It is the curling movement of the snail's shell, rather than the snail's own motion, which is indicated here. But the picture could represent other things; it is far from being a realistic portrayal of an animal. The fact that it is called *The Snail* is secondary to the enjoyment of the gay colors and bold design of the shapes.

Henri Matisse (1869–1954). *The Snail*

In this way, it has something in common with Calder's sculpture of the whale. Both are lively abstractions. Neither are descriptive of the animal from which they take their title, but both suggest that animal by abstracting from it certain characteristics. For the whale, it is a leaping or sailing movement, fins, and the hint of mass. For the snail, it is the circular shape of its shell.

51

Pablo Picasso (b. 1881). Plate from *Histoire Naturelle* by Comte de Buffon, Martin Fabiani, Paris, 1942

Movement can be indicated by drawn lines, as in this drawing of a running ostrich by Picasso. All the lines in the background follow the direction of the bird's movement, suggesting his speed.

Antelope. Mali: Bambara tribe

Antelope. African

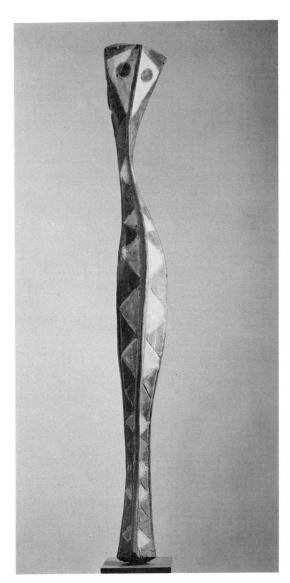

Snake. Guinea: Baga tribe

Emphasis on the direction of a line in a static object such as sculpture can give the sculpture particular expression. These African wood sculptures all have in common a sense of elongation, of being stretched out. The long, thin quality gives to the snake and to each of the antelopes its own personality.

Persian manuscript illumination (*Ibn Bakhtishu*), 13th century

54

Dish. Asia Minor, 16th–17th centuries

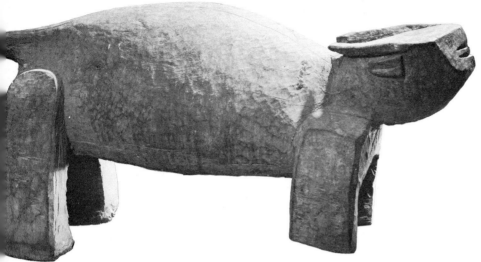

Bovine. Mali: Bambara tribe

Hippopotamus. African

Animation in art, as we have seen, is achieved when subject matter seems endowed with some quality of life. The portrayal of animals in attitudes which suggest they are talking to each other, as in this Persian manuscript page, is a good example. But animation can result from other, less human activities. The young blue deer on the Arabic dish seems to have three feet off the ground, as if he were leaping or prancing about in frolic.

Sculptural shapes can express humor as well as animation. These animals—a bovine, a hippopotamus, an unknown Mexican

55

Animal. Mexican

beast, an armadillo, and a hedgehog—have in common a round, full quality of form that we usually find appealing and often amusing in both real animals and sculptures of them.

Armadillo. Peruvian

Hedgehog vessel. Greek

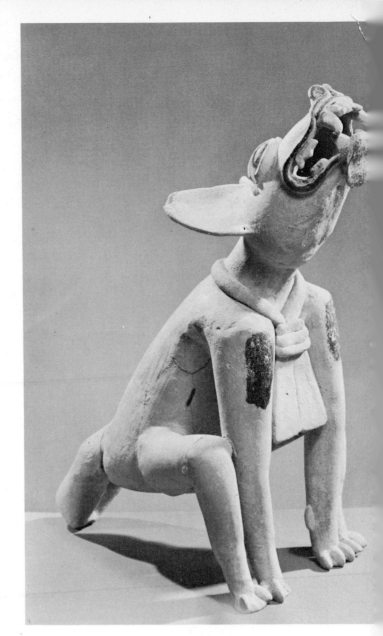

Coyote. Mexican

Frog. Mexican

The animation of these creatures, competing in their silent chorus, results from both their shapes and their open-mouthed activity. Because each is howling so energetically, each seems vigorously alive.

Gargoyle. French, 14th century

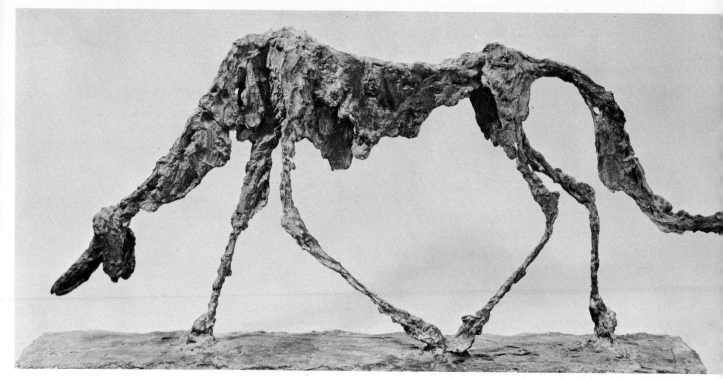

Alberto Giacometti (1901–1966). *Dog*

The nature of each of these dogs is implied by its own particular shape, form, and attitude. The dogs range in age from the third century to contemporary times. There is a very old Chinese dog, a Gothic French dog, and a modern dog by Giacometti, an artist of Swiss descent. Each one has a different personality. Which would you choose? Why?

The qualities for which we choose one equally fine work of art over another are as personal as the qualities for which we might choose a real dog as companion and pet. Each of the artists represented here has tried to express a different, particular quality about a dog. Because each has limited himself to a simple idea, no single portrayal can be expected to satisfy *all* our feelings about dogs. Everyone responds to different qualities at different times and in different moods.

Tastes vary as much in art as in anything else. There is no right or wrong in art. The more we look at works of art, the more selective our taste becomes and the easier it is for us to say why we think one thing is better, more pleasing, or more expressive than another.

Dog. Han Dynasty, China, 3rd century

Gothic *cul de lampe*. French

Coin. Greek, 5th century B.C. (enlarged 5 times)

The material used by the artist influences to a great extent the portrayal of his subject. This Greek metal coin is very stylized. The details of the owl's feathers are suggested by only lines and dots. The coin, like the Greek coin of the crab (page 46), is a *bas-relief*. If the owl could step off the coin, he would appear flat and cartoonlike because of his two-dimensionality and the "short-hand" portrayal of the details.

The very careful, detailed painting by Albrecht Dürer, on the other hand, is realistic. By means of gentle brushstrokes of color, the sixteenth-century German artist has suggested the soft plumage of the owl. The feathers are not indicated by hard lines, but presented to us by the artist's technique of painting layer upon layer of tiny strokes of color.

62

Albrecht Dürer (1471–1528). *Little Owl*

The owls on the next two pages were made by still other techniques, each technique and material lending special characteristics to the portrayal. Although the owl from Colombia is metal, it is executed in the round, unlike the *bas-relief* coin opposite. The Colombian owl was made as a decoration in gold and is only 4¾ inches high. It is stylized in a different way than the Greek coin. The goldsmith

63

Owl. Colombian

lines suggest pot feathers

target

Pot. Costa Rican

Round

Pot →

who made this little owl was a master craftsman in a precious metal. He could work as minutely and as decoratively as his skill and the nature of the metal would allow. The feathers on the front of the gold bird are indicated by an open or *filigree* pattern of circles; the wings themselves are smooth metal. The face and tuft on the top of the owl's head are simplified, while a fine chain of gold around the face and around each eye adds a note of elaborate decoration. The stylization here depends upon patterned adornment, or a decorative quality which the Greek coin does not have. The coin was made to be used as money, not as decoration.

The painted ceramic owl is a pot from Costa Rica. If we look carefully we can see that the head of the owl can be removed like a cap. He is decorated with straight and curved lines. The lines on his wings suggest feathers, as do the lines on his tail. The large owl eyes are suggested by two double-line arcs, or semicircles, one above and one below the round eye itself. On top of his head, circles form a design like a target. The feet do not resemble claws at all, but he is easily identified as a bird—and his owlish eyes tell us what kind of bird.

The third owl is a drawing from a twelfth-century manuscript. The manuscript was a "bestiary," or a book about beasts written and illustrated in the Middle Ages to describe the natural

English manuscript, 12th century *Awkward, Medeival*

properties of real animals. The artist tried to make the owl as realistic as possible, but he has given it a human face! The eyes have eyebrows, the beak is like a nose, and there is a human mouth. It gives the owl a curious expression indeed.

The Greek coin, the golden owl, and the pot are all objects originally made to be used for a specific purpose. In each case, the figure of the owl makes the useful object more attractive. The medieval bestiary drawing was supposed to show readers of the bestiary what an owl looked like. In that sense, it too was made for a specific purpose: illustration.

The Dürer painting, while it tells us much more about an owl than the rather awkward medieval drawing, was not made specifically for purposes of illustration. It was made as a work of art, and it has great value to us for that reason.

The Unicorn at the Fountain. Unicorn Tapestries, French or Flemish, *ca.* 1500

Unicorn
dips his horn
in the fountain
to make H2O
safe for other
waiting animals

66

O Unicorn among the Cedars
To whom no magic charm can lead us.
White childhood moving like a sigh
Through the green woods.

W. H. AUDEN, *New Year Letter*

Magic
charm against
poisons

embroidery

Stag. Coptic textile, *ca.* 11th century

Christian

In fable and mythology, the unicorn is a symbol of purity. It is considered a relative of the stag and other horned animals. According to the bestiaries, the horn on the right side of the stag's head is useful for healing diseases and calming fevers. Either horn, right or left, can be burned to keep away snakes, serpents, and dragons.

The single horn of the unicorn is also magic. It is a charm against poisons, particularly arsenic. It has the power to purify water which a dragon has made unsafe with its venom. In the sixteenth-century Unicorn Tapestries we can see the unicorn dipping his horn in the fountain to make the water safe and pure for the other animals who wait to drink.

To the right of the unicorn is a stag. The animal is more realistically depicted in the medieval tapestry than in the embroidery above, which is from the Christian, or Coptic, culture of Egypt. In the embroidery we can see a smaller stag within the larger one, as well as several stylized birds.

Embroidery is the handmade ornamentation of woven textiles by stitching with a needle in heavy colored thread. Embroideries are often made by individuals for personal use, either to adorn clothing or to decorate the home. Embroidery can be made in a variety of techniques and designs. It can be used to decorate the border margins of tapestries.

The unicorn, the magical beast, had the body of a horse, the tail of a lion, the hoofs of a stag, and a single horn in the center of his forehead. Sometimes his horn was as long as four feet. It was so sharp that it easily pierced anything the unicorn attacked.

67

Master of the Playing Cards. Stag and unicorn

Some medieval writers say that the horn was movable and that the unicorn could battle with it like a sword. The unicorn was an enemy of the elephant, and often fought with him. He could wound the elephant in the belly with his horn, thereby defeating the largest of all the beasts.

The unicorn was said to have a horrible howl. He was very strong, and so swift-footed that no hunter could catch him. At the same time he was extremely gentle and good-natured.

There was one way in which the unicorn could be caught. The unicorn was so attracted to all things pure that he would surrender himself gladly to a pure, innocent young girl. It was said that the huntsman on the trail of a unicorn would lead a young girl into the woods and leave her there alone. Eventually the unicorn would

English manuscript, 13th century

come to her and meekly put himself at her mercy. Placing his head in her lap, he would unsuspectingly fall asleep.

Then the treacherous huntsman would appear from his hiding place to capture the beast as it lay quietly at the girl's feet. It was a prize catch for the hunter because the wondrous horn was very highly treasured. The horn was not only magic; it was also an emblem of the unicorn's goodness just as his white color was a sign of his purity.

The unicorn we know in western art and mythology is a relative of a Chinese creature called the Ch'i-Lin. The Ch'i-Lin had the body of a deer, horses' hoofs, and the tail of an ox. Like the unicorn, he was of a very kindly nature and walked gingerly to avoid treading on insects.

69

Chinese embroidery. Ming, 14th–17th centuries

The beast on this Chinese tapestry square is a Ch'i-Lin, Oriental cousin to the unicorn.

Dragons are fabulous animals usually found in hot lands, although it is said they also appear occasionally in more moderate climates. They belong to the serpent or snake family. Contrary to general opinion, dragons in some countries are often very friendly.

Opposite is a Japanese dragon with the body of a serpent, made as a crest for a metal helmet in the nineteenth century.

Dragon. Japanese, 19th century

In ancient Japan, serpents and dragons were numerous. Once, legends say, a dreadful eight-headed dragon from a certain part of Japan had terrified a village by eating the daughters of an old man and woman, one by one for seven years until there was just one daughter left. When it came time for the eighth daughter to be eaten, the great Susano-o, god of the crops as well as god of thunder, rain, and storms, came to challenge the dragon.

Susano-o changed the last remaining daughter into a comb and stuck the comb into his hair. Then he filled eight rice bowls with strong rice wine and waited. When the greedy dragon appeared, each head went straight to one of the bowls of wine. The dragon was soon very drunk, and he fell soundly asleep. Susano-o quickly cut the monster into pieces. He then changed the girl back into her natural form, and she and the god Susano-o were married.

In China, dragons were considered powerful and helpful friends.
※ Some of them lived underground and humped up their backs to make hills. Others lived in the sky and controlled wind and rain. Still others lived in the seas. Each of the four dragon-kings of China was said to live in one of the four seas which the Chinese thought lay around the earth. Each of the dragon-kings lived in a crystal palace and commanded an army of fish, crabs, and crayfish to

71

Dragon. Chinese

protect him. A police force of marine animals enforced the laws of his bottom-of-the-sea kingdom.

Above is a Chinese mythological beast modeled from terra-cotta.

Dragons were often a test of courage and strength for heroes in mythology. One of the tasks of Herakles was the destruction of the

Seven-headed dragon. Spanish manuscript, 15th century

Hydra, a giant serpent with nine heads. The breath of this dragon was so poisonous that anyone who came close to it was instantly killed. Herakles finally destroyed the Hydra by setting a forest on fire to burn off its heads.

During the Middle Ages in Europe, dragons were thought to give off great heat as they flew through the air. According to the medieval bestiaries, the dragon, contrary to popular belief, did not always have poison in its tail or jaws; it often killed its victims by strangling them in its coils.

Here is a seven-headed dragon from a medieval bestiary.

73

English embroidery, 17th century

This far from fearsome dragon shows us how tame the beast could appear in a homemade embroidery. The dragon, embroidered in a variety of stitches, was part of the decoration of a set of bed hangings made in England during the second half of the seventeenth century. The Greek leopard opposite has also been "tamed" and colored blue. He, too, was part of a bedspread, made on the island of Skyros, during the seventeenth century.

Greek embroidery, 17th century

Leopard. Nigerian

Paul Klee (1879–1940). *Young Beast*

No bestiary would be complete without lions, tigers, and leopards. This bronze leopard is African. Glaring at him is a mustached Spanish lion, painted in the early thirteenth century. He was painted on a wall as a *fresco,* a technique whereby dry pigments or colors are worked into wet plaster.

76

Lion. Spanish, 13th century

Reliquary, 13th century

The bronze lion is a thirteenth-century reliquary, or container for sacred religious objects. If we look carefully we can see the hinge just above his mane. What seems to be the lion's tail lifts up to reveal a hollow body. Facing him is a playful beast drawn by Paul Klee, a twentieth-century Swiss artist.

Coptic textile, 5th–8th centuries

Animal themes have been woven into textiles for a long time. In the Odyssey, Homer, who lived about 1000 B.C., describes a hunt woven into a tapestry. Decorative animals were often embroidered on robes. Textiles are not easily preserved, and old ones are very rare. This one is from the Christian culture of Egypt and dates from the eighth century or earlier.

The Flemish manuscript and Paul Klee's drawing offer two versions of a similar idea, done seven centuries apart—one in the thirteenth century, the other in our own.

The medieval bestiaries say that if a tigress finds a cub stolen from her lair she will immediately pursue the thief. But if the thief tosses a mirror on the ground behind him, the tigress will see her own reflection in the mirror and think it is her lost cub. Then the thief may escape safely with the real cub. This medieval manuscript, in which the tiger is said to be speckled, tells the story.

The drawing by Klee is a beast, perhaps a tiger looking at itself in a mirror. Possibly the artist obtained the idea of a beast intrigued by its own mirror image from a medieval bestiary. The drawing is made entirely of enclosed shapes without shading.

78

Flemish manuscript, 13th century

79

Paul Klee (1879–1940). *Beast and Mirror*

Rembrandt Van Rijn. (1606–1669). *Elephant*

80

Rembrandt Van Rijn (1606–1669). *Camel*

Rembrandt van Rijn, a Dutch painter who lived in the seventeenth century, was one of the greatest masters in the history of art. He was a superb draftsman, often beginning a drawing directly with pen and brush without preliminary guiding lines. Here is Rembrandt's chalk study of an elephant—fresh and energetic in its quality of line. We sense the bulk of the huge animal even though the lines are delicate and feathery.

Rembrandt was a keen observer of nature. His pen and brown ink drawing of a camel might be compared to the life-like watercolor of the owl (page 63) by Albrecht Dürer, who lived almost a century earlier. Attention to certain, selected details as, in this drawing, building up by washes and many fine strokes of the pen the tuft of hair which follows the curve of the camel's neck, is evidence of Rembrandt's devotion to the truth of his subject. This devotion to his own vision was an artistic integrity which Rembrandt shared with Dürer. Rembrandt was a prodigious artist. Besides about 650 paintings and 300-odd etchings, he produced more than 1500 drawings.

81

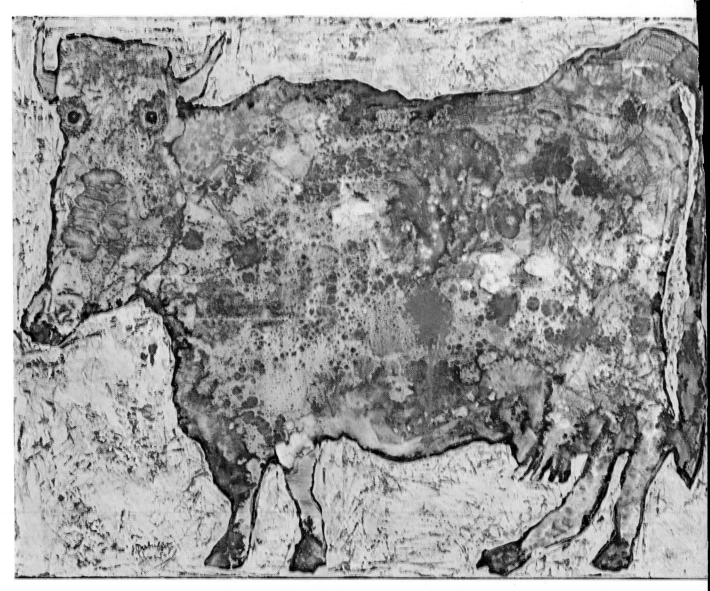

Jean Dubuffet (b. 1901). *The Cow with the Subtile Nose*

Here the contemporary French painter Jean Dubuffet has abstracted the simple outline shape of a cow. As animals may be combined to make new ones in man's imagination, and therefore in his dreams and in his art, so may cows be purple.

The subtly changing surface texture and color of this painting make it something more than an outlined study of a cow. Our pleasure in the painting is increased by the addition of wit in the artist's drawing of the animal, but the painting becomes in itself an object for us to enjoy. The paint is heavily applied, giving the surface a rich and beautiful luster.

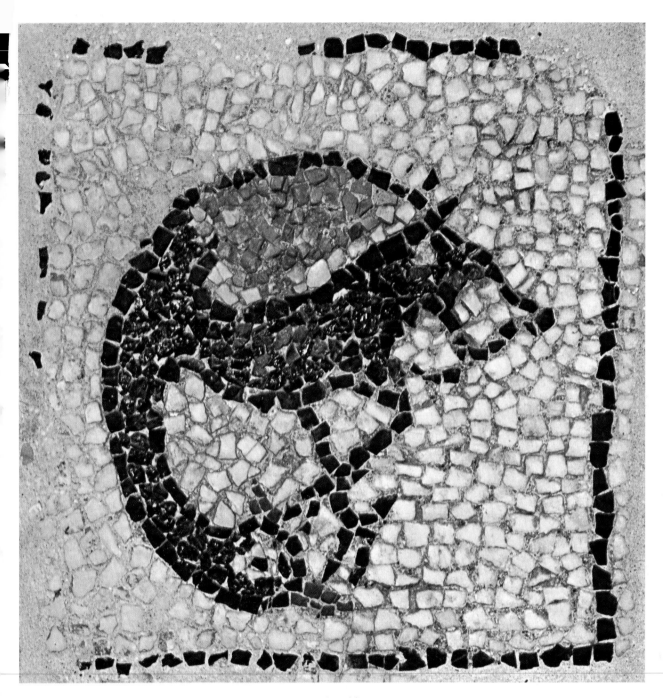

Bird. Greek mosaic, 5th century, B.C.

This long-necked bird, designed to decorate a house in fifth-century Greece, is portrayed in a medium called *mosaic.* Mosaic is made by placing pieces of colored glass, or chipped stone (as here), in a wet substance such as mortar, which when it is dry will hold the bits of color in place. The bird forms a "C" shape, his head bent down to his feet.

83

Marionette. Mali: Bambara tribe

The horses presented here have in common a unique simplicity of form and a clarity of line. What are the qualities which give the horses special expression?

The horse's head is African. It is extremely simplified. Strips of metal are attached to an elongated shape of wood on top of which are carved two ears. This horse was used by the Bambara tribe of Mali in Africa as a marionette.

The clay horse is Japanese, dating from between the fourth and sixth centuries A.D. It is called a *haniwa* figure. *Haniwa* means "circle of clay." The details of the horse are made with strips of clay. The eyes are simply two round holes punched through the head. The *haniwa* horse is hollow, and the nose as well as the legs are hollow cylinders, or tubes. *Haniwa* figures were placed into the soft ground around graves. This is one reason the legs are hollow: in order to be placed into the ground so that the figure could remain upright. Sometimes these figures formed a kind of low fence, encircling the tomb.

The carved, wooden horse is contemporary, by Alexander Calder. If we look carefully we can see how the pieces of carved wood are fitted together. The body and neck of the horse are elongated or stretched out, the head directed forward. This exaggeration gives the horse a "streamlined" look.

Horse. Japanese *haniwa*, 4th–6th centuries

Alexander Calder (b. 1898). *Horse*

Greek embroidery

Compare these horses to the birds on pages 40 and 41 and to the fish on page 49. By studying many examples of sculpture we can begin to understand that artists may make many variations of a single animal.

This Greek tapestry takes advantage of the decorative possibilities of the shapes of the figures—men, animals, birds—and foliage. Compare the wobbly legs of the horse to the sculpted legs of the Greek horse and the Chinese T'ang horse. Of the three, the metal Greek horse seems most prepared to run. The contrast of the

86

Horse. Greek, 5th century, B.C.

Horse. T'ang Dynasty, China, 7th–10th centuries

large flanks with the narrow body emphasizes the muscular strength
of the animal, and suggests his fleetness. The T'ang horse seems
sturdy in comparison, but not as fleet. All three of these horses have
an alert quality.

87

Horse and rider. Greek, 5th century, B.C.

Compare, finally, these three fine horsemen: one ancient Greek, one African, and one by a contemporary artist. The long snout and narrow body distinguish the Greek horse from the others. It is modeled in clay. The African horse and rider is carved from wood. The horse and rider by the modern Italian sculptor, Marino Marini, is cast in bronze.

What simplifications make the Marini bronze similar to the African horse and rider? (Also compare the body of the Marini horse to

88

Horse and rider. Mali: Dogon tribe

Marino Marini (b. 1901). *Horse and Rider*

the Chinese T'ang horse.) There is a similarity in these three sculptures which goes beyond subject matter.

Vastly different cultures have produced these works of art over a period of more than two thousand years. We have seen how various the images of something as basic as the sun can be. Here, on the other hand, is evidence that occasionally art can cross all boundaries of culture and time and express a common concept through the use of similar forms.

WARRIORS

And Arthur and his knighthood for a space
Were all one will, and thro' that strength the King
Drew in the petty princedoms under him,
Fought and in twelve great battles overcame
The heathen hordes and made a realm and reign'd.

TENNYSON, *Idylls of the King*

Warrior. Greek, 5th century, B.C.

History and legend abound with colorful accounts of courageous and memorable deeds. Many civilizations have had real heroes whose brave and daring exploits are both celebrated and exaggerated in legend and in art.

What the heroes have in common, whether they are real men or legendary figures, is courage and stamina, whatever the nature and value of their pursuit. In Greek stories the philosopher Socrates, who really lived and was martyred for his teaching, is as much a hero as Achilles, the valiant conqueror of Troy. The lyre player Orpheus, listed among their heroes by the Greeks, was not famous for warlike adventures, but for his amazing musical talent. Other Greek heroes were venerated and are still remembered today for their wisdom or cunning rather than for deeds of physical daring or brute strength.

Most often, however, heroes in both history and legend have been the personification of physical strength and courage. They are usually warriors, and very often they are as bad-mannered and egoistic as they are brave.

The best-known of the Greek heroes is Herakles, who was an athlete so glorious that none could defeat him. He is portrayed in Greek art as a man of great muscular power. Herakles was said to have founded the Olympic games, a festival of athletic competitions. He was revered as a demigod, and in his day was a great destroyer of monsters.

91

Herakles wrestling with Antaeus. Greek vase

Probably more grounded in truth are the heroes of the Trojan War: Achilles, Hector, and Patroclus, whose stories survive for us in Homer's poem, the *Iliad;* and the adventurous Odysseus of Homer's *Odyssey.* The stories of these men—their nobilities and their human faults—encouraged a kind of hero cult in the ages that succeeded them, and their exploits are often told in pictures painted on Greek vases. One of Herakles' contests was his wrestling match with the giant Antaeus. Here we see the bottom of the vase.

The heroes of the Middle Ages in Europe were the courageous knights of legend. Like the stories of many of the Greek heroes, there is probably some truth to their histories. Knights were mounted men who were permitted to bear arms in the service of their king or feudal superior. The word "chivalry," which is derived from the French word *cheval,* or horse, described the code under which they lived and fought. These horsemen, clothed in mail or armor, and

English manuscript, 13th century

armed with a lance and sword, were soldiers of fortune who fought and skirmished for their pay. Yet they were also men of "chivalrous" and lofty spirit.

The institution of chivalry was designed to modify the horror and brutality of the warfare in which the knights took part, and through its code, they were encouraged to be valorous and generous to their foes. An important part of the concept of honor was the demand that the opponents be evenly matched. Above two knights engage in combat with their swords while their horses seem to be clinched in a draw. One knight has apparently unhorsed the other and jumped down from his own horse to meet his opponent on even terms. This line drawing is from a thirteenth-century English manuscript.

Knights showed off their skills in jousts or tournaments. In the simpler competition of the joust, the warriors fought with only

93

their lances, the object being to knock the opponent off his horse. Various weapons were used in tournaments, and greater courtesy was observed, but neither competition was a harmless game.

Although tournaments and jousts were often held for the revenge of past injuries or insults, they often served other purposes. When the "good and gentle knight" Ipomydon fell in love with the lady of Calabria, he could not declare his love, since he was then serving the lady disguised as her servant and he had sworn never to reveal his identity. When eventually the lords of Calabria insisted that the lady marry, she agreed to accept the knight who proved most worthy in a three-day tournament. Of course Ipomydon was the gallant victor, and so won the lady of his heart.

When Richard the Lion-Hearted was crowned king, he held a tournament and took part in it himself in disguise. In this way he discovered which of his knights were his worthiest. Some of these he took with him to the Crusades.

Knights did go to war. Thousands of them risked their lives in the battles of the Crusades. The Crusades were begun to save Eastern Christendom from Moslem rule. By the time they ended, nearly four centuries later, the whole of Eastern Christendom was under Moslem rule.

According to the legends surrounding them, the knights of King Arthur's Round Table lived lives of brave and magnanimous activity. It is thought that Arthur was born about the end of the fifth century and that he was the general of certain royal armies fighting in South Britain. Whatever their basis in history, the stories of King Arthur and his knights have been told so many times that they are now immortal.

Knights were well-known in Arthurian legend for their bravery in killing dragons. They rode off in quest of a dragon's lair, which was usually to be found high among burned rocks above fire-scorched valleys. Once he had challenged the dragon, the knight fought with his spear, usually wounding the dragon first to weaken it before the real contest began. Even as it lay dying, a dragon was a menace to the courageous knight who slew it. After Tristram had dealt the death blow to the terrible dragon in Ireland which had devoured people and laid waste to the land, the dragon breathed such flame and poison into the air that Tristram's shield melted from the blast. Tristram himself was half-poisoned by the dragon's breath, and was only restored to health through the healing magic of Queen Isolde.

cotidie ab agno superatur. qui abeius
pacientia confunditur.

INCIPIT DE AGNO ET BESTIA SVPERATA

n decem reges cu agno pugnabunt.
& Agnus uincet eos. qin dns dnorum
est et rex regũ et qui cu eo uocati et sũt
electi et fideles. Et dicit michi. haec
uides ubi mulier sedet. ppls et turbe
sunt. et gens. et lingue. et dece cor
nua que uidisti hii odio habent & de
serta eã facient et nuda et carnes eius
commedent & ipsam comburet igni.
ds enim dedit incorde eorũ facere senten
ciam eueridare regnũ suũ bestie. usq;
dum finiatur dicta dñ. Et mulier
quã uidisti est ciuitas magna que habet
regnũ sup reges terrae.

Dix Rois. French manuscript, 12th century

French sarcophagus, 12th century

SIR EGLAMOUR

Sir Eglamour, that worthy knight,
He took his sword and went to fight:
And as he rode both hill and dale,
Armèd upon his shirt of mail,
A dragon came out of his den,
Had slain, God knows how many men!

When he espied Sir Eglamour,
Oh, if you had but heard him roar,
And seen how all the trees did shake,
The knight did tremble, horse did quake,
The birds betake them all to peeping—
It would have made you fall a weeping!

But now it is in vain to fear,
Being come unto, 'fight dog! fight bear!'
To it they go and fiercely fight
A live-long day from morn till night.
The dragon had a plaguy hide,
And could the sharpest steel abide.

No sword will enter him with cuts
Which vexed the knight unto the guts:
But, as in choler he did burn,
He watched the dragon a good turn;
And, as a yawning he did fall,
He thrust his sword in, hilts and all.

Then, like a coward, he to fly
Unto his den that was hard by;
And there lay all night and roared.
The knight was sorry for his sword,
But, riding thence, said, 'I forsake it,
He that will fetch it, let him take it!'

SAMUEL ROWLANDS

During the early Middle Ages in Japan, the period called the Kamakura, warrior heroes emerged because it was bravery and audacity that succeeded, usually drenched in blood. It was a time of continuous warfare. The counterpart of the European code of chivalry was the cult of death, honor, and loyalty of the Japanese warriors, or *samurai*.

In the struggles for power in the twelfth century, a leader named Nobuyori and his men attacked and burned the Sanjo Palace, seizing the retired but still-powerful Emperor Go-Shirakawa. On the following pages is part of a long picture scroll, called an *e-maki,* which narrates the story of this famous battle.

Although the reproduction is cut in half so there will be no details lost, the *e-maki* itself is a long, continuous strip of scenes, one scene flowing into the next. It was painted in brilliant colored inks and made to be unrolled by hand and read from right to left, the story unfolding in space and time.

In the illustration the principal part of the palace is already enveloped in flames. The horsemen led by Nobuyori gallop furiously after those who are trying to escape.

Heiji Monogatori. *Burning of the Sanjo Palace* (detail). Japanese, 12th or 13th century

100

Bishamonten. Japanese Kamakura period, 12th–14th centuries

The artist was interested in maintaining a certain realism, and by looking at the faces and gestures of the warriors we can discover which are the defeated and frightened, and which are the attacking warriors trying to look fierce. The quality of the lines is immensely varied. There is a crispness to the drawing and a carefully controlled use of color which gives it great elegance, a coolness as if the artist were somewhat detached from the story he is telling.

As we look at the picture we realize that the artist wished to show disorder and confusion, but there could have been no confusion in his mind. There are a great many people in the painting, but everything is carefully drawn in its place. The composition is controlled, with all of the relationships important to the whole.

Our eye jumps from red patch to red patch, taking in the great activity and agitation of the battle scene. Intensifying and dramatizing the activity is the blazing and triumphant fire. The fire is an example of Japanese stylization of line. The flames are drawn, one by one, in disciplined and careful curves which seem to caress the palace which they consume. Although there is a great deal of smoke, the flames do not really look capable of emitting heat. What we see is a stylized representation of a large and destructive fire.

This dramatic figure, carved from wood, is from the same period of Japanese art as the Heiji Monogatori scroll. Compare the crisp, hard-edged, yet delicate flames of the magnificent fire in the scroll to the curving, carved lines in this figure's sleeves and billowing skirt.

This is Bishamonten, the armored Guardian King of the North. His scowling face and the vigor of his stance are typical of the art of this militaristic period in Japan.

The Japanese scroll on the next page is designed to hang on a wall. It shows the *samurai* Benkei, standing with fierce expression, holding a lance with a curved blade. Benkei is drawn with heavy, black brush lines. If we look very carefully we can distinguish one brush line from another, and follow the movements of the artist's hand as he designed the figure.

The Japanese writing below Benkei is called calligraphy. If we imagine some of these lines enlarged to the same size as the figure, we can see how similar the drawing of Benkei is to the calligraphy around it. Compare these free-flowing lines with the more controlled lines of the Heiji Monogatori *e-maki*.

Opposite Benkei, and portrayed in a very different manner, is a Peruvian warrior woven into tapestry. The weave of the fabric

Benkei. Japanese scroll

shrunken head (handwritten annotation)

Peruvian embroidery

limits the naturalness and freedom of line, and the figure seems stiffly depicted in comparison to Benkei. In one hand he holds a staff or lance; in the other, a shrunken head. On his headdress is a white face which resembles a skull.

Warrior, Greek, 5th century, B.C.

These three warriors can be analyzed to some extent on the basis of the shapes they contain. Although they are all made of clay, they are from different epochs and different civilizations.

The Greek warrior with the shield and four horses was probably made as a toy, about the fifth century B.C. Since the craftsman who made it wanted the four horses to move with the chariot and driver, he put the horses on *top* of the chariot. The four wheels are clay disks, or solid flat circles.

The warrior with the long skirt is a *haniwa* figure from the age of ancient burial mounds in Japan. It is much older than the scrolls. Compare it with the *haniwa* horse on page 85. Like the horse, the warrior is based on a hollow cylinder shape. The skirted body of the warrior is a cylinder pinched in the middle. If it were pinched together until the sides of the figure met, the cylinder would become two cones placed point to point. A cone is a rounded, solid triangle. The top of the *haniwa* warrior's helmet is roughly in the shape of a cone.

The seated Mexican clay figure with the staff is also built on a cylinder shape. His head pokes out from the round top which forms a sort of collar. We know this figure is a warrior because of his helmet, which is like a hollow cone, the flair at the bottom and the roundness of the top making it bell-shaped. He is from the Colima culture in Mexico, and was made in the sixth century.

104

Warrior. Japanese *haniwa,* 4th–6th centuries

Warrior. Mexican, 6th century

Warrior. Mexican, *ca.* 600

We have already seen that sculpture can often be analyzed according to the geometric forms it contains. Compare these warriors with the birds on pages 40–41. The modern marble bird by Noguchi is based on a cylinder. The body of the painted bird from New Guinea is a fat circle. We have found similar simplifications of shape in the *haniwa* and Mexican warrior figures.

Artists often generalize natural forms in terms of simpler ones. It is not difficult to see geometric forms such as cones, cylinders, and spheres (solid, three-dimensional circles) in natural objects. Consider a cone-shaped tree on a cylindrical trunk with spherical fruit or berries among its leaves. Artists rarely just replace the natural, irregular shapes with the simpler, elementary ones, however. Instead they use the simpler forms to heighten the special quality they see in the original.

The warriors illustrated here have in common the fact that they are both frontal sculpture; that is, they have been designed with the area of major interest from the front view. (This is less

Jaina figure. Mayan, 7th–10th centuries

true, for example, of the *haniwa* and the Mexican warriors on page 105.)

The two clay figures are from ancient Mexican cultures: one from the Remojadas culture in Veracruz (about 600 A.D.), and the figure shown in color from the classic era of Mayan art on the island of Jaina (about 600–950 A.D.). The difference between the re-

Bronze plaque. Nigerian, *ca.* 1400

strained realism of the Jaina figure and the cruder simplification of
the Remojadas is striking. Neither is more than ten inches high.

The bronze plaque is from the Benin culture in Nigeria, Africa.
It was probably made about 1300 or 1400 A.D. As in the earlier
Jaina figure from another continent, there is naturalism and a re-
fined control of the material.

THE SKY AND THE NIGHT

Look at the stars! Look, look up at the skies!
O look at all the fire-folk sitting in the air!
The bright boroughs, the circle-citadels there!
GERARD MANLEY HOPKINS, *The Starlight Night*

Woodcut from the *Chronique
de Nuremberg,* 1493

How easy it is to gaze at the vastness of the sky and understand the
magic and wonder that it held for primitive man. Especially at night,
when the absence of the sun's light allows us to see billions of stars
many billions of miles away, we can vividly imagine the awe of
men who tried to bring the infinity of the sky within their understanding through religion and the symbols of mythology and art.

The sky is our constant companion. It is our silent witness. We
cannot yet alter its appearance or change the weather. The sky's
various moods can, however, affect *us.*

Primitive man believed that fate was decided by the gods whose
home was in the sky. For him, the moon and stars, with the
almighty sun, determined not only the days, the seasons, the tides,
and the climate, but the fortune of his own society as well.

Most ancient cultures thought that before the creation of gods
and men, the earth and sky had been united into one whole. Then,
at some moment, a powerful force—some thought it was the winds
—pushed the sky away from the earth to let in light. Like an inverted bowl or roof, the sky then spanned the earth.

In the Babylonian myth, the god Marduk divided Chaos (the
goddess Tiamat) into two halves "as a man splits a fish," suspending
one half up high to become the heavens, and spreading the other
half beneath his feet. The sky became a kind of vault which reflected the sun during the day but was dark at night.

109

In the oldest Greek mythology, the force was the goddess Eurynome. She simply arose from the disorder of Chaos and in order to have something to stand on, she divided the sea from the sky. Then she danced upon the waves.

The Roman creation story, as related by Ovid, explained the division in terms of weight. The fine air of the heavens was separated from the coarser air which men breathe. The completely "weightless" fire rose to the highest zones of the heavens, while the heavy earth settled and was surrounded by water. The stars, which had been obscured by Chaos, now began to shine and became the abode of the gods.

For some tribes in Tahiti the force that separated sky from earth was a big plant which enlarged the space as it grew. Whatever the cause of the separation, underneath and within the sky lived the gods; on the earth lived man.

It is extremely difficult to depict or even suggest the vastness of the sky. Early men knew that the sky, like the sun, could not be completely explained by a visual representation of what they thought they saw. But the sun presented a shape to them, and therefore—whatever their beliefs about its rising and setting—the sun itself could be symbolized by a simple disk. The whole sky was not so easy to portray.

The Chimu tribe, who lived on the north coast of Peru about 1100 A.D., solved the problem by placing many symbols of the sky together in one composition. This Peruvian painted cloth shows us a sky god holding above him a double-headed snake which also represents the sky. We can see what is probably a sun in the upper left corner. It has a face, upside-down. Below it is a star-like figure which seems to be spinning in space. The painting is the Chimu tribe's representation of the whole sky, a picture of several familiar images portrayed together in an attempt to make the unknown sky more understandable.

Compare this painted cloth with the painting of the figure with the sun in his stomach on page 31. In the same way that Miro's painting suggests to us the world of the artist's imagination, this Chimu depiction of the sky suggests the vivid imagination of primitive culture. Both paintings have in common the use of a unique and personal visual language which makes their imagery poetic.

In some cultures the sky god (or goddess), being the ruler of the universe to the extent to which it was known, was held in greater veneration than the sun god. The sky god was often con-

Peruvian cloth, 12th century

sidered the parent of the sun. In pagan Slavic mythology the sky gave birth to two children: the sun and fire. Slavs addressed prayers to the sky as the supreme being, calling it Svarog. Svarog controlled lightning (thus fire was born) and with this power to produce flames he relighted the sun every morning.

But as the father of the sun and infinite, the sky god presented a problem of visual portrayal to all cultures. Sometimes the sky god was represented in the "borrowed" form of an animal, but usually, like many other gods, he was portrayed in human form. Zeus, Greek king of the gods and ruler of the sky, is depicted as a man of superhuman proportions. Zeus threw thunderbolts like Svarog, and on the few occasions when he appeared to men in his real form, he blazed with the light of the sky where he lived. The god Anu of ancient Mesopotamia, usually shown as a warrior king, took advantage of his position as god of the sky to command all the stars as his soldiers.

The ancient Egyptians had several concepts about the sky. One idea was that the sky was a body of water through which the sun sailed every day in its riverboat. Another was that the sky was a roof

111

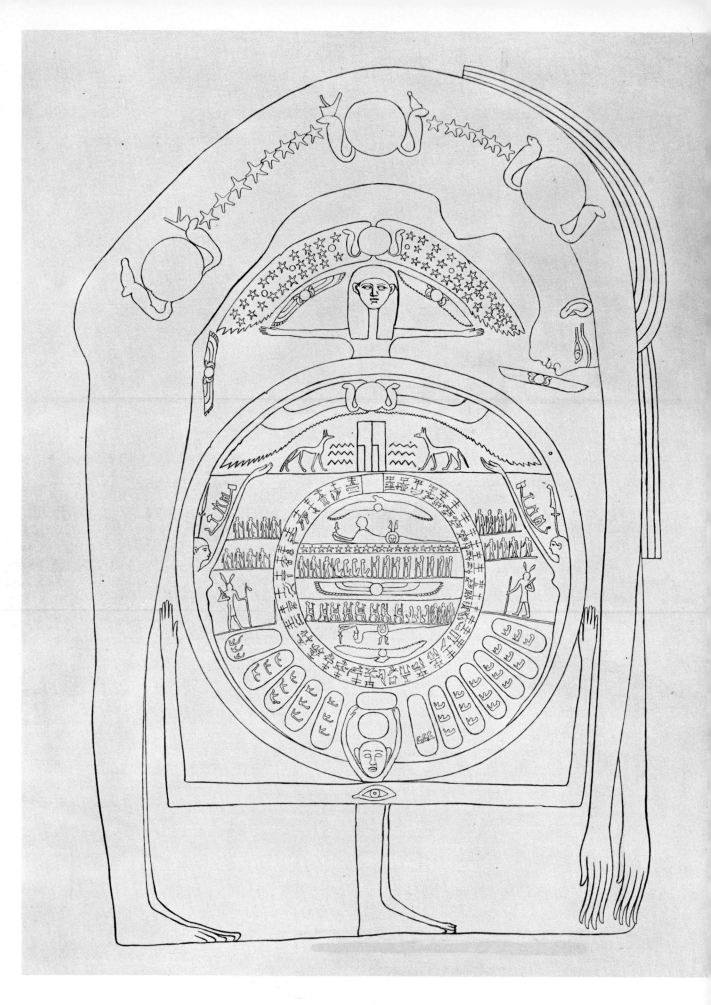

Sarcophagus of Uresh-nofer. Egyptian. Drawing from cover

held up by four pillars. Sometimes the sky was symbolized by the picture of a "heavenly" cow. At other times it was shown as a vulture, or a falcon, as we have seen, which spread its wings to protect the earth. Sometimes the sky was depicted in the female form of the goddess Nut, who was lifted up on the day of creation by the god Shu to form the star-strewn sky. Before that she had been locked in embrace with the earth, Geb. Her body, sprinkled with stars, is usually shown bending over the earth, sometimes supported by Shu.

This drawing of a sarcophagus shows the goddess Nut in her personification as the sky. Her body bends in an arch over the whole universe as the Egyptians conceived it. Here—in a symbolic sense—she *is* the sky just as, for the Greeks, Helios was the sun. Directly underneath her body are star-covered falcon wings, which also represent the sky.

Stars have always played an important role in mythology. In the drawing of the sarcophagus they decorate the body of Nut and are shown in the most common shape for a star—with five points.

There are believed to be approximately 110 billion stars, including our own sun, forming what is called our Galactic System. The remotest extension of these stars—those which we can see with telescopes, some only very faintly—is the Milky Way. The stars are separated by vast distances from one another and from our sun. Since the stars are too far away from us to present a disk for our contemplation, as the sun does, the conventional five-pointed symbol indicates the "twinkling" aspect of starlight which is all we can see of a star.

The Eskimos consider the stars little lakes in the black "grasslands" of the sky. The ancient Sumerians, who lived in the valley of the Tigris and Euphrates, believed the Milky Way to be a flock of heavenly sheep. For the ancient Chinese, the Milky Way was a great river in which the moon and stars washed before making their sparkling appearance in the evening sky.

The reign of the early Greek kings was often influenced by happenings in the sky. During the eighth year of a king's reign, the magistrates or officials of the Spartan kingdom would choose a clear and moonless night and watch the sky carefully. If there was a meteor, or "shooting star," it was assumed to be a sign that the king had done some wrong and he was suspended from his duties. If a star fell, so did the king.

Before scientists studied why comets move as they do and reappear when they do, comets were also considered indications of

113

some dreaded occurrence. Before the conquest of England by the Normans in 1066, Halley's comet appeared in the sky. Later, the comet was considered to have been of great significance and was interpreted as having been a warning to the English.

In the detail of the Bayeux Tapestry we can see the court astronomers pointing up at Halley's astonishing "bearded star." Nearby is King Harold of England himself, being told of its alarming appearance. This tapestry, probably done in the early twelfth century, was embroidered by craftsmen or perhaps the women of the town of Bayeux in France. It tells the story of the conquest of England in "comic strip" fashion. Since many people could not read, this was one method of recording popular history. The "legends" or writing near the pictures is Latin.

In order to understand more about the gods and forces in the sky, men studied the sky. In 4000–5000 B.C., the Babylonians carefully catalogued the stars and could predict their movements and relative positions. The stars generally represented gods or were identified with them, and were thought to rule man's destiny. For this reason, men consulted the star-priests to find the positions of the stars on their birthday in order to have secret knowledge about the future. The priests kept records of heavenly phenomena on slabs of clay. Every night they noted the position and brightness of the stars and the moments of their rising and setting.

The Babylonians had discovered regularities in the movements of the sun and moon by the beginning of the second century B.C., and could probably predict eclipses. Gradually the science of astronomy developed. Now, understanding more about natural processes in the sky, we are no longer afraid of comets and falling stars.

Bayeux Tapestry (detail). French, 12th century

Filamentary nebula in *Cygnus*

But modern knowledge of the nature of the sky and stars does not mean that for poets and artists the fabric of the heavens no longer suggests imaginative material.

Myths are not simply relics of early cultures. Although we may be less frightened than primitive men by the sight of a meteorite or comet, when we gaze at the sky we ponder things that concern the life and death of man on our own earth.

I could not sleep for thinking of the sky,
The unending sky, with all its million suns
Which turn their planets everlastingly
In nothing, where the fire-haired comet runs.
If I could sail that nothing, I should cross
Silence and emptiness with dark stars passing,
Then, in the darkness, see a point of gloss
Burn to a glow, and glare, and keep amassing.

And rage into a sun with wandering planets
And drop behind, and then, as I proceed,
See his last light upon his last moon's granites
Die to a dark that would be night indeed.
Night where my soul might sail a million years
In nothing, not even Death, not even tears.

JOHN MASEFIELD

115

This painting of the moon by the Russian-born painter Nicolas de
Staël is poetic and personal. The uneven shape of the moon seems to
hang heavily over the horizon, looming above the landscape. The tiny
vertical line underneath the moon gives great space to the painting,
space that seems to extend in all directions. It is like the string of a
balloon from which the heaven-bent sphere has just broken away. Yet
the string is taut, as if it still held its massive charge. The line both holds

Nicolas de Staël (1914–1955). *The Moon*

Paul Klee (1879–1940). *Star Over a Rock*

the suspended moon in balance, and releases it to its weighty position in the sky. This painting has more in common with the Van Gogh painting on page 119, than with the Klee drawing above, even though a globe dominates them both. With de Staël and Van Gogh we sense the passion of the artist and his involvement with his subject.

Paul Klee has drawn what he calls a "star over a rock." No one has ever really seen a star as a disk because the stars (except

117

for our sun) are too far away. The rocks here are abstracted shapes. They seem to be supporting the "star." The star seems almost to be a part of the rocks, but since it is round we can distinguish it from them. This is an intellectual approach to the depiction of an element in the sky, unlike Van Gogh's highly emotional approach. Also it is a "flat" design. It does not suggest space to us. The line of the drawing winds along describing the outlines of the rocks and the star, like the path of a restless walker.

For the Dutch painter Vincent Van Gogh the whole sky had movement, as we have seen in his portrayals of the sunlit sky. He describes a night sky in a letter to his brother:

"One night I went for a walk by the sea along the empty shore. It was not gay, but neither was it sad—it was—beautiful. The deep blue sky was flecked with clouds of a blue deeper than the fundamental blue of intense cobalt, and others of a clearer blue, like the blue whiteness of the Milky Way. In the blue depth the stars were sparkling, greenish, yellow, white, rose, brighter, flashing more like jewels . . . opals you might call them, emeralds, lapis, rubies, sapphires."

In *The Starry Night,* on the next page, Van Gogh has given us his vision of a living, dynamic sky. The moon in the upper right corner glows with a yellow warmth. The stars are painted with warm yellow centers surrounded by dozens of tiny brushstrokes in cooler, whiter tones. The stars seem to be coming closer and closer to us through the night air like the headlights of approaching space cars. The clouds swirl between them.

Color areas in this painting are sharply contrasted, the trees standing out in silhouette. The intensity of the color suggests the artist's involvement with the landscape he was painting. Here, as in his other paintings, we sense that Van Gogh's art is truly symbolic of his own personal and deeply felt experience.

In the painting there is more sky than land, but Van Gogh gives us a sense of life on earth as well as energy in the sky. He has painted little houses in the foreground of the painting. They have glowing windows which suggest that there are people inside, cozy and safe while the sky above them as well as the trees and mountains around them pulse with activity.

The cypress trees to the left curve and move with the same gesture as the clouds above. The vertical line created by the tallest cypress tree, however, acts as a gentle brake to the intense movement of the painting. So does the steeple on the church, which is like a miniature shadow of the cypress. We feel there is a distance be-

Vincent Van Gogh (1853–1890). *The Starry Night*

tween the cypress and the church steeple, because we know that the steeple is as big as the cypress tree. This is an illusion which creates space in the painting.

While the church seems to be some distance away, the sky seems very close. Van Gogh has exaggerated the clouds, moon and stars because of his deep feelings about the sky. Because he had the genius to transpose his emotion and insight through his painting skills into art, we recognize and are moved by his vision.

119

Robert Indiana (b. 1928). *Moon*

The moon is portrayed above by the contemporary American sculptor, Robert Indiana. The title is stenciled on the wooden column which forms the sculpture. If we look closely we can see that the artist has drawn symbols of the four major phases of the moon. (Phases are positions of the moon as we see it in the sky in its relationship to the sun and earth.) The artist has placed four wheels on either side, perhaps to suggest the revolving of the moon about the earth and the annual

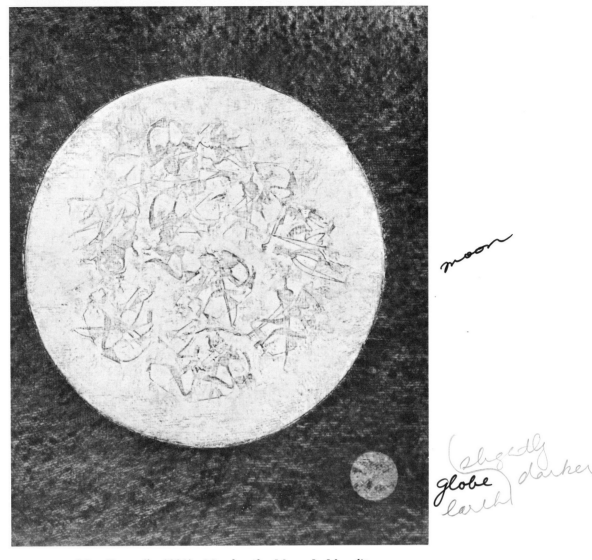

moon

(slightly darker)
globe earth

Max Ernst (b. 1891). *Monday the Moon Is Moonlit*

revolution of both earth and moon around the sun. Above the wheels is the number "4," representing the moon's new, first quarter, full, and last quarter. The symbol for the new moon is a black disk (actually a colored disk in the sculpture itself). It is at the bottom of the column. Above it is the symbol for the first quarter, above that the white disk representing the full moon, and at the top we see the last quarter of the moon.

The moon has been the subject of several poetic paintings by the German-born (now French) Max Ernst. Ernst is usually referred to as a *surrealist* because of his interest in fantasy. In the painting above, the light disk represents the moon, and in the lower right corner, slightly darker in value, is a globe which might be the earth. Scratches or veins, like mysterious writing, appear on the surface of the moon. While intellectual in that it is the artist's idea of how the moon might appear from the sun, the painting has emotional content and thus a different appeal than Indiana's symbolic sculpture.

121

Henri Matisse (1869–1954). *Christmas Night*

Finally, the French artist Henri Matisse has chosen one of the most magic nights in the year as the theme of this colorful *collage,* a study for a chapel window. It is called *Christmas Night.* The composition was made by cutting and pasting papers which were painted under the artist's supervision. The stars dance about among the cut-out clouds while the background sky changes from blue to green to orange and even red. It is a happy celebration. The *collage* is long and narrow and curved at the top, following the shape of the stained-glass window. It is the artist's homage to the wonder of the starry sky on a gay Christmas night.

Season inherits legally from dying season;
Protected by the wide peace of the sun, the planets
Continue their circulations; and the galaxy

Is free for ever to revolve like an enormous biscuit;
With all his engines round him and the summer flowers,
Little upon his little earth, man contemplates

The universe of which he is both judge and victim . . .

W. H. AUDEN, *Commentary*

PHOTOGRAPH CREDITS

INDEX

Page numbers followed by an asterisk (*) indicate illustrations.

125

127

ABOUT THE AUTHOR

Beryl Barr is a well-traveled young American artist living in Paris. She teaches for and is Associate Director of *College Art Study Abroad,* a program of art study directed by her husband, Roger Barr, a sculptor, and founded by the Barrs in 1963.

Under her professional name, Beryl Barr-Sharrar, she has exhibited paintings in three one-man shows and numerous group shows in Europe. In 1964, she was the first American recipient of the *Prix Le Franc* for painters under thirty.

Born in Virginia, Mrs. Barr received a B.A. degree in philosophy from Mount Holyoke College in 1956, and an M.A. degree in art from the University of California, Berkeley, in 1958. She was a fellowship student in 1955 at Yale-Norfolk, the summer school of the Yale School of Design. She went to Paris in 1959 under the auspices of a Mount Holyoke College Fellowship for travel and study abroad.

Mrs. Barr is co-author of *The Artists' and Writers' Cookbook,* published in 1960. *Wonders, Warriors, and Beasts Abounding* is her first book for young people.